Erin Olson has written a must-read book for every Christian especially in our current world climate! She wrote *Spiritual Orphans* as a reminder that our calling as believers is to bring Christ to every person, not just the ones we think are worthy. Erin wisely states, "Our current crisis can only be undone by ushering spiritual orphans into the presence of the Almighty God." It's time to lay down our divisiveness and join in the call Jesus left with all believers: "and you will be my witnesses to the ends of the earth" (Acts 1:8).

—CECILIA BACON
AUTHOR, GOING HOME: A STORY OF RUTH AND NAOMI

Sharing the love of Jesus with others is a responsibility for every believer. Erin breaks down exactly what that means in a way that tears apart our preconceived notions of who we are to extend that love toward. This book is timely and much needed for reaching today's generation of spiritual orphans.

—VIRGINIA GROUNDS
AUTHOR, SPEAKER, AND TEACHER
MAJESTICINSPIRATIONS.COM

SPIRITUAL ORPHANS

SPIRITUAL ORPHANS

ERIN OLSON

Visit the author's website at www.sandalfeet.org.

International Standard Book Number: 978-0-9993544-7-6
E-book ISBN: 978-0-9993544-8-3

19 20 21 22 23 — 987654321
Printed in the United States of America

Contents

Contents

Foreword

If you knew me, knew my wife (which, by the way, is the author, Erin Olson), and if you knew our journey, you would know the God-sized miracle you are reading right now.

First, I am not a reader, and have barely read a whole book in my entire life. And yet, here I am writing a foreword for my wife's fourth, and maybe most important, book. Only God!

Never in a million years would anyone have thought that the two of us, from difficult backgrounds and far from God, would end up living for Jesus with all our hearts. Only God!

We were spiritual orphans—rescued and adopted by God because two very special people cared enough to love us, pray for us, and tell us about Jesus.

So, for my wife, writing this book was easy (easy for me to say) because she writes her story—and mine—and the story of millions of people all over the world that is still being written. Millions of people need someone to introduce them to a loving Father that will never let them down.

If you want to know such a Father or if you want to be challenged to help others know Him, please read this book. It will change your life!

Thank you, my sweet wife, for never giving up on people.

—SCOTT OLSON
CEO, Pathway Healthcare

Acknowledgments

This book has taken much longer than I ever thought it would take. Perhaps it is because of the seriousness of the issue. Maybe a little of it was fear of what people might think because people have varying opinions about who God loves and who He doesn't and how Christians should address the issue. Whenever I navigate hard topics, I know it is the Holy Spirit who gives me perspective and guidance on how to handle God's Word in our modern world. I can never thank Jesus enough for sending the tremendous blessing of the Holy Spirit to all believers.

I also want to thank my supportive husband. He leads quietly, and even when we don't agree, he extends me grace and does his best to see me how Christ sees me.

My three children are my biggest supporters and most vocal accountability partners. If you want to know anything about the Erin that exists behind closed doors at home, just ask them.

Lastly, I want to thank all my friends and family who encourage me to keep writing and doing what I can from my little corner of the world.

I wrote this book not just to reach the lost but to help Christians live out the command Jesus left us with: love God and love others. We are called to reach *all* people. It's not always easy, pleasant, or perfect. But if we want to change the condition of this world, it starts with you and me showing people who their Father is and how much He loves them.

—ERIN OLSON

Introduction

Sixty seconds. Sixty seconds is how long the US Coast Guard says a drowning person can struggle on the surface of the water before submersion.[1] Once a person is submerged under water, well, we know what the potential outcome might be—death. A "silent killer" is how many describe drowning. Why? Because our respiratory systems were designed to breathe, not call out for help. Drowning people aren't on the surface long enough to inhale, exhale, and form a word. They are gasping for air. One statement stood out to me as I read through the US Coast Guard's *On Scene* journal: "Drowning people cannot wave for help."

As I look at the world today, I feel like I am looking at drowning victims everywhere, and they cannot wave for help because they are simply trying to survive. We are no longer a society of deep thinkers, contemplating the things of this world or focusing on the One who created this world. Instead, we mostly remain on the surface of everything including our relationships, our faith, and our values.

All this was in my mind when it came to the cover design for this book. I wrestled with what I had selected after showing it to some people, who initially said it was disturbing and offensive when they looked at it. Others

1

said that it piqued their interest. After a recent conversation I had with a pastor friend, I thought about changing the cover entirely. However, after reading the statement, "Drowning people cannot wave for help," I just knew the cover design is the message I hope to convey in this book.

During my wrestling with the cover art and some other issues my pastor friend brought up, I thought about changing the cover to fire (representing hell), but a hand emerging from fire representing hell seems so final to me—so hopeless. However, there is hope because Jesus lives.

You and I can make a difference today wherever we are to be a part of pulling people from death to life. We have that power in us because of the Holy Spirit in us. But, you and I must choose to activate this power. The life-preserver we throw out is Jesus. Jump overboard by yourself and the drowning person could take you down.

Let's not do this thing alone. Let's understand our position in His kingdom and what our purpose is. Let's remember His grace. Let's live to exalt His glory.

What we are experiencing in these days is nothing short of a crisis. *Oxford Dictionary* defines *crisis* like this:

- A time of intense difficulty, trouble, or danger.

- A time when a difficult or important decision must be made.

- The turning point of a disease when an
  important change takes place, indicating
  either recovery or death.[2]

How one views the current crisis depends on their worldview. Many blame crooked governments, big business, culture, global warming, liberalism, war, refugees, or any combination. However, the very things people choose to blame are not the thing or things causing our crisis. Our crisis is not what we witness in the physical realm; our crisis lies within the spiritual realm.

The crisis in our world is serious. The most serious is that there are people dying every day who did not know God, who didn't confess Jesus as their Lord and Savior, and who were never born again as believers of Jesus Christ (John 3:3). Let me be clear from the outset, I do not believe all people are God's children. I believe we are all created by God, but because of the fall of mankind, at birth, we are separated from Him (Rom. 5:12). For those who ask about infants and young children (and people with special cognitive needs) going to heaven, honestly, I do not know how God handles all of that. It is not clear in Scripture. I'd like to think they do. However, I can't find the verse where Jesus said that only people over the age of six years old need Him as their Savior. All I do know is that it is important children learn about Jesus and know Him personally as soon as possible.

We are spiritual orphans (people without the Father) until the moment we choose through faith to accept the free gift of salvation offered to every single person because of the birth, death, and resurrection of Jesus Christ (Eph. 2:8–9). Only after accepting God's free gift of salvation is a person adopted into God's family (Eph. 1:4–5). There is a gravity to the fact there are people walking around who could be eternally dead at any given moment.

The pull of this world is not toward God but away from God. Jesus overcame this world (John 16:33), and He's the only One who has done this. The rest of us are left to endure what is in this world. Jesus warned us about what would take place. Our hope lies not in this world but in eternity toward which we can set our expectations. This hope is available only for those who believe in Jesus's death, burial, and resurrection, which was for the sole purpose of fulfilling prophecy and standing in the gap for all mankind as the ultimate and final sacrifice. Yet, with all that Jesus did, this world will still have trouble. Why? Because there will always be people who are spiritually separated from the Father.

Several years ago, I had a series of dreams. In the first dream, I stood at the top of a large rock protruding out of the ocean. There were people around me, as well as people ascending the rock. However, what I remember most about this dream was the people in the water who were in distress. Their hands were above the water as their bodies sank below the surface. Some were struggling. Some were trying to get on the rock, but something kept knocking them off. In my dream, I stood on the rock thinking, "How can I help them? What can I do?" I felt helpless.

A few years after this dream, I was assigned to read

a book on evangelism called *Share Jesus Without Fear*[3] for one of my seminary classes. I wasn't more than a few pages into the book when the author described a dream he had that was eerily similar to the one I mentioned above. It got my attention, and that image of people struggling in the water has stuck with me since.

Who were the people in the water struggling in my dream? They were people who had not yet believed in and accepted Jesus as their Lord and Savior. I call them "spiritual orphans" because they are without God the Father. My prayer is that people will see the lost not as completely lost but see them the way Jesus sees them—as spiritual orphans in need of adoption by God, their heavenly Father.

Why does it matter if there are people who are separated from the Father? It matters because the actions and behavior of people who do not know and fear the Lord are thrusting us deeper and deeper into crisis. We can't expect those who do not believe in Jesus to think like He does, care about people the way He does, or do the things Jesus told people to do, because they don't know Jesus (1 Cor. 2:14).

So how can we help stop the madness? We step in. We take action. We take responsibility for the spiritual orphans. We engage them with the hard conversations. We tell them about Jesus's love. We help them do life. We offer godly counsel (like a mentor would). Just as God expects a mother and father to train up a child (Prov. 22:6), as Christians, we should also take this command seriously for His children (those who are and those who will be His). If an earthly parent fails to physically care for a child, the child needs an adoptive parent. So, too, are spiritual orphans in need of spiritual care and adoption.

The term *spiritual orphan* may not ever cross your mind, but it should. If the Holy Spirit desires to use us to reach unbelievers, why would we choose not to be used? Our current crisis can only be undone by ushering spiritual orphans into the presence of the Almighty God. Please let it not be said of our generation as it was of the prophet Ezekiel's generation:

> I looked for someone among them who would build up the wall and stand before me in the gap on behalf of the land so I would not have to destroy it, but I found no one.
>
> —EZEKIEL 22:30

Are you willing to stand in the gap for this generation? My prayer is by the end of this book your heart will be moved toward love for the spiritual orphans God places in your life.

Ever since I had my first child in 2002, a desire was birthed in my heart to have a large family. Around the time my oldest child turned one, I was eleven weeks pregnant with our second child, and I miscarried. That was one of the hardest days of my life. I remember being so overwhelmed with grief. I clung to my young son as I rocked him to sleep that night and cried. I knew I wanted more children, but it didn't happen quickly. My husband and I tried for over a year and a half after the miscarriage to have another child. It seemed impossible. During this long season of my life, adoption crept into my heart.

However, after many long months, I discovered I was pregnant again. We had a healthy baby girl in August 2005. Even though I had two healthy babies, it didn't take long for the desire toward adoption to surface again. I sought out ways in which it might be possible, but doors did not open.

A little over a year later, I discovered I was pregnant with our third child, and we delivered a healthy son in September 2007. We had known before I had our third child that I would most likely not go down the path of getting pregnant again. I had easy pregnancies, but they were hard at the same time. I gained close to sixty pounds with each pregnancy. The toll of carrying three babies and that much weight within a five-year period did not agree with my body. We knew without a doubt this would be the last biological child we would have. I'm pretty sure my baby son wasn't even a week old when I began to dream about the possibilities of adoption again.

I didn't come by motherhood naturally. In fact, I barely managed through the first few years of motherhood, and my oldest child took the brunt of my parenting missteps. The whole idea of having a large family, including the thought of adoption, wasn't something that had been on my heart my entire life. I spoke to adoption agencies and researched open countries. I read books on adoption and continued to dream about the possibilities for years.

One night—January 29, 2011, to be exact—at the end of a very long and emotional day of parenting, I cried out to God asking Him for special revelation about my purpose and His plan. Let me set the context before I share this word with you.

I'm a mom who doesn't have everything figured out. As a young mom with newborn babies, I had absolutely no clue what I was doing. I had never even held a newborn baby before I had my son. Most days, I felt like a failure. I yelled too much. I felt like I was rushing my children's years away by always looking forward to their first day of school. I found very little peace in the mundane of everyday homemaking and childrearing even though I loved my babies fiercely. I loved snuggling them, and I loved watching them grow, but simply loving cute, cooperative babies isn't exactly the same as loving trying toddlers. It's also not the same as loving preteens and teenagers who think they know more than you, and it certainly isn't the same as loving adults who have a different view or lifestyle than you.

I want you to know all this about me because God's response to me that January night was a bombshell. It rattled me in my insecurity, but it also gave me confidence because I know His plan will always come to pass if I yield to His will.

After crying out to God that evening, His response was clear, "You are a mother. You will be a mother to all My children who are hurting, sick, scared, and lonely." It wasn't an audible voice, but it was the kind of voice you can feel deep down in your soul.

When I asked Him how I would know who these

children were, the Holy Spirit whispered, "You will know it when you see them. You will see it in their eyes."

I didn't know what God meant that day, but I knew it was important enough to write it down in my prayer journal. It was a nugget God dropped on me as a revelation of what was to come.

Throughout the years, adoption doors continued to close. I put the adoption process on hold and instead, sponsored children hoping that would fill the void. It didn't. It gave me some comfort knowing we were helping with their sponsorships, but the desire to adopt never went away.

In early 2014, the desire to adopt increased tremendously, and I took action (if you sense that the word *I* meant I went before my husband in all of this, you'd be correct—it's not something I recommend). I chose to adopt from Haiti, hoping we might be able to adopt one of the young girls we had been sponsoring in the orphanage (that's the idea I used to get my husband on board). An international agency helped us, we gathered all the documents required for the dossier, and underwent our home study.

I don't know what it was about the home study that absolutely terrified me. Deep down inside, I think I was afraid there was a possibility that someone who didn't know us had the power to say whether we were fit to be parents (even though we had biological children of our own). Perhaps the home study is easy for people who have led easy lives, but for my husband and me, this was not the case.

Our childhoods were complicated. The whole thing

brought back a lot of painful memories and issues I don't like to often discuss or think about. And on top of all that, I started getting nervous about parenting children who had lived through some of the things we experienced. Honestly, we were just barely keeping afloat parenting our biological children without overwhelming bouts of fear and doubt.

Shortly after starting the adoption process, we found out that the little girl we were sponsoring wasn't eligible for adoption. Ultimately, my husband and I couldn't get on the same page about adopting someone else. I understood his hesitations. I prayed and prayed. I asked God to either move the adoption forward or remove the desire from my heart. A couple of years ago, I wrote the adoption agency and told them we were not moving forward and that I would love for them to donate the money we had in our account to help another family adopt. To this day, adoption has not left my heart. It's only over the last few days I've realized why the desire is there.

God doesn't want me to adopt one orphan. He needs me to be available to and make a case for all spiritual orphans.

So many twists and turns have led up to the above revelation, and all of it goes back to that word on January 29, 2011. God didn't say I would be a mother to three or four or five. He said I would be a mother to *all* His children in need. *All* is a big number. How big? I have no idea.

Yes, there is an orphan crisis in the world today, and

many might say this answer is a cop out. Surely we could adopt just one child and encourage others to do the same. I would, and I do. I'm so thankful to have friends who have answered this call. The Christian church alone could rid the world of orphans if every Christian would adopt just one orphan. My adoption story may not be over yet (only He knows), but the message the Holy Spirit has put on my heart is so much bigger than the millions of physical orphans—those who have lost one parent and/or both parents—who exist around the world.

There are billions of spiritual orphans—young and old—who have no connection with their heavenly Father. Regardless of what we experience in the physical realm, nothing compares to what we lack in the spiritual realm. This thought is where the Holy Spirit has me right now. I was trying to manipulate something in the physical (physical adoption) God is trying to manifest in the spiritual (spiritual adoption). We can't manufacture what the Maker has already created. We—all of us—have a need for God, the Father. Even if some like to mess with it, it's His perfect order. Spiritual disorder contributes to physical chaos. We aren't the first generation who has had to deal with this problem, but I am praying and seeking, and asking you to consider being part of a generation who can change the spiritual atmosphere through obedience and love.

What did the early church do? What was its focus? Its focus was to share the gospel message. Its focus was to speak about Jesus to everyone who would listen. People flocked to hear this message. People did some crazy things, and often countercultural things, to hear from the disciples who had walked with Jesus.

Are people banging down your door to hear about Jesus? Do people know you've been with Jesus or do they know you go to church but don't act like you care about people at all? If we want to live the abundant life Jesus came to give believers (John 10:10), then isn't it safe to say that our actions, or lack thereof, have some bearing on the world around us? As believers, Jesus gives us eternal life. How can we hold that in? How can we not share it with the hurting, hopeless, and broken world?

As we share about His love to those who don't yet know Him, we are bringing glory to His name. As more spiritual orphans are adopted into God's family, the world gets a little brighter. Oh, how this would affect our everyday life for the good. I'd love to see a day when there is less war, less crime, less sadness, less anger, and more righteousness. I'm not only referring to heaven; I'm also referring to now.

Jesus came to give life. There are too many losing their lives because they are right now not in the book of life. Jesus isn't about to tell God that He knows who they are, but you and I can do something about it. We can become a mighty army leading people to Jesus instead of being the stumbling blocks some have become because of opinions, biases, theology, and differences. If God was searching the earth right at this very moment, would He see in you a heart prepared to reach those whom no one else might want to? I hope so. Let's find out.

Chapter One

REMEMBER WHERE YOU CAME FROM

D O YOU REMEMBER the moment you first felt shame or embarrassment in the church? I do. It is hard to put into words, and if I tried to explain it to you, you'd probably look at me like I was a little crazy. But let me just say, as I look back and connect all the dots from that day to the present day, it all makes sense to me. It was in a weird moment on a Maundy Thursday. I was thirteen years old, and I remember being so excited to attend the Holy Week events with my grandmother. As I sat in church that day, something happened. Satan got into my head and began whispering things to me like, "You are not welcome here. You will never be."

That whisper knocked me off course. My foundation lacked substance to begin with, so his words washed away anything I felt toward God. I hesitate to say Jesus because, honestly, I didn't know Jesus at the time. You see, Satan messes with our minds because he doesn't have access to our hearts; Jesus does. Everything Jesus asks us to do focuses on our hearts. The thoughts I had were blurry because Satan was weaving his web of deception deep into my mind and eventually, my soul. For years, his lies washed me out to sea. I grabbed onto anything that looked like it would sustain my life only to find out that everything fell short of giving me the life I wanted.

As teen years progressed and I became a young adult, I knew in my heart I needed to be in church. However, every time the thought of church came into my mind, Satan pressed in further: "You are not welcome here. You will never be." I thought for sure the "church people" would figure out I wasn't fit to be in their church. They would find out what I was up to, who I hung out with, and (gasp) that I had tattoos back before tattoos in the church were hip.

When I moved to Dallas at the age of twenty-four, I wanted to find a church in my new city but I couldn't muster up the energy or the courage to walk into a church without knowing anyone. It would be over two years before someone extended an invitation to attend church. And even though I finally stepped foot into a church, I still didn't feel like I was good enough to be in that place. I still feared people would figure out my sin—for some reason I assumed they were all without sin—and I didn't want to go down that path. So, I remained guarded and distant for several more years, and I bought into Satan's lies. His whispers became louder: "You are not welcome here. You will never be."

Satan knew church is where I wanted to be, and ultimately

> *Very few people have been judged into life-change. Many have been loved into it.*[4]

where I would feel most at home. I was a spiritual orphan in need of adoption, and I needed a forever home.

Sin separates us from a holy, heavenly Father. The Old Testament required animal sacrifices and other sacrifices to be made for sin to be forgiven. Only through the shedding of blood could a person be cleansed from sin. However, what Christians face today is not that sin separates us from God (because believers will sin after salvation), but the repetition of cherished sin—unconfessed sin, known or unknown. Psalm 66:18 says, "If I had cherished sin in my heart, the Lord would not have listened." When we sin (even after salvation), we drive a wedge between our Father and us. We can't live lives of disobedience to God and expect the world to be OK.

When Adam and Eve sinned against God by eating of the forbidden fruit, their sin resulted in expulsion from the garden. (See Genesis 3.) They lost fellowship with the Father. Fortunately for Adam and Eve, even though they lost the close fellowship they once enjoyed, God never left them completely. They still knew who their Lord was. God blessed them with two sons, Cain and Abel. Abel was the good son. Cain was not-so-good. Abel gave his best to God while Cain only gave some to God (Gen. 4:3–4). When God confronted Cain about his anger toward his brother, God warned Abel, "If you do what is right, will you not be accepted? But if you do not do what is right, sin is crouching at your door; it desires to have you, but you must rule over it" (Gen. 4:7). The answer to be accepted by God was not to sin.

Cain, it turns out, could not rule over sin. His sin ruled him, and he ended up killing his brother, Abel. Abel's murder angered God. His response to Cain was, "You will be a restless wanderer on the earth" (Gen. 4:12). Cain chose to follow in the footsteps of his parents and allow sin (going against God's instructions) to rule over him. He left the Lord's presence and moved east of Eden (Gen. 4:16). Anytime anyone moved east, it always meant moving away from the presence of God. When the temple in Jerusalem was first constructed, the holy of holies was located toward the back of the western wall. Even within the temple, the farther a person moved east, the farther away one moved from the presence of God. One writer said about "east," "Positive, godly things come from the east. But traveling to the east is a bad thing."[5] Another writer stated, "As humanity moves further away from their founding, their chaos evolves from the naivety of shame, hiding, and blame shifting of Adam and Eve to a whole organized system built upon the moral foundation of sin."[6] Cain moved east. The Tower of Babel was east of Eden. Sodom and Gomorrah were east. Farther and farther away from where God first dwelt.

Cain's family was wrought with sin and rebellion against God. Cain's pride caused him to name a city he founded after his son Enoch (Gen. 4:17). Enoch's name meant "dedicated."[7] Cain's great-great-great grandson, Lamech, married two women—something not originally designed by God. This was just another example of pride and rebellion against God. If that wasn't enough, Lamech also murdered a man and announced what the punishment would be for someone who killed him (Gen. 4:23–24). Lamech had heard family stories about his great-great-great-great-grandparents who also believed they were on the same playing field as God, thanks to that little, slippery snake. Sin and rebellion led Cain out of the presence of God, and his choices left his future generations wandering and outside of God's presence. God gave Cain the antidote to sin—do what is right—but Cain chose his way over God's way.

Cain and Abel represented the first example of God's family being divided. Both Cain and Abel were created by God, yet Cain voluntarily chose to disobey and abandon God. Abel, on the other hand, chose to obey God and do what was pleasing to God.

Unlike physical orphans, people are spiritual orphans not because their heavenly Father does not love them or cannot care for them. They are spiritual orphans because they don't know or love their Father. When it comes to interacting with spiritual orphans, we need to be aware of this. There is a difference between a prodigal and an orphan.

An orphan, specifically a spiritual orphan in the context of this book, is someone who does not know or believe in Jesus as their Savior and therefore cannot be reconciled to God the Father. A prodigal is someone who knows Jesus and has been reconciled to God but has chosen to move away from the presence of God and do life on their own terms. For the purpose of this book, I am talking about people who are spiritual orphans because I am concerned with people's eternity. Prodigals (if they truly have accepted Jesus as their Savior) are like Cain. They are creating havoc for themselves and people around them because of disobedience, but if they truly gave their lives to Jesus, their eternity is secured, and hopefully, they will come to their senses and return fully to the Father during their lifetime.

A prodigal's eternity with God is secure, but a spiritual orphan's is not. There are lots of prodigals contributing to the chaos in our current world. They need help too. In a lot of cases, people may actually be spiritual orphans even if they identify as prodigals.

Cain was a prodigal not just because he sinned against God, but because he didn't own his sin. Instead of repenting and asking for forgiveness, God drove Cain out from His presence and cursed Cain because God alone knew the condition of Cain's heart. Cain acknowledged that he would be a "restless wanderer" all his days. (See Genesis 4:10–16.) Had Cain softened his heart toward God, things may have turned out so much differently for him, his offspring, and even for us today. The sad part is, Cain's children found themselves cut off from God because of Cain's choices. They were spiritual orphans because of Cain. As the years progressed, Cain's descendants weren't walking with God. It wasn't until Adam and Eve's third child, Seth, grew into an adult and had a child that people first began to worship the Lord by name (Gen. 4:26). I am so thankful we are no longer held to the sins of our parents as it relates to our relationship with God.

When we look at lost people only as prodigals instead of orphans, we see rebels instead of spiritual orphans unaware of their spiritual family. Prodigals bow their neck at their Father while the spiritual orphan doesn't even know their Father. It is hard to reach a stubborn, prideful person like Cain, but know that it is not always impossible. It is also difficult to reach someone who thinks their life is totally within their own control. However, it is God, through the Holy Spirit, who draws people to Him.

Do you ever wonder how bad it must have been for God to flood the entire earth? Cain made some bad choices, but come on, were they really *that* bad? If Cain existed in today's culture, how would he rank? Cain's family consisted of adulterers and murderers, and who knows what else. Eventually, the sons of God took many beautiful wives. Some scholars say the sons of God were fallen angels, some say the sons of God were descendants of the righteous Seth, and some say the beautiful women were daughters of Cain's descendants. Regardless of exactly who they were, the mere fact the sons of God took many as their wives thrust these descendants to a whole new level of sinfulness.

Seth, as I mentioned earlier, was Adam and Eve's third son. He was born after Cain killed Abel. Eve was convinced God granted her another son in place of Abel (Gen. 4:25). It was as if just speaking words of affirmation over baby Seth caused him to grow to be righteous just as Abel had been righteous. Ultimately, Seth had many children and had a large legacy. Seth's great-great-great-grandson Enoch walked so closely in fellowship with God that one day he disappeared because God took him (Gen. 5:24).

Enoch didn't experience death. Enoch's great-grandson was Noah. According to Scripture, "Noah was a righteous man, blameless among the people of his time, and he walked faithfully with God" (Gen. 6:9). Some translations say that Noah was the only blameless person living on Earth at the time. Noah was righteous when everything around him was anything but righteous.

God saw what the world had become—corrupt and violent—and He chose Noah as a part of His solution. God's solution to the corruption and violence was to wipe out all the living creatures, including people. He chose to spare only Noah's family (him, his wife, their three sons, and their son's wives), and two of each animal (one male and one female). (See Genesis 6:9–7.)

In a span of one thousand six hundred and fifty years, people went from living in the Garden of Eden in complete fellowship with God to being completely wiped from the face of the earth.[8] Because Adam and Eve introduced sin into the world, and many chose to follow a pattern of sinful living, all but Noah and his family were destroyed. God didn't offer up a chance to repent. He was done with them.

Are we any different from the people in Noah's day? How does our generation hold up to the scrutiny of God looking over the earth? What do you think God says about the things we think, imagine, and do? Oh, how our generation must grieve the Spirit and break God's heart.

I wonder if any of Seth's descendants tried to reach Cain's descendants with truth? Or were they so hardheaded like Cain, their ears and hearts were closed and hardened? God Himself had a conversation with Cain about how to rule over sin, and for Cain, that didn't seem to make a difference. He voluntarily chose to leave the presence of God because of his lack of repentance, and consequently, his offspring, never returned to the presence of God. Because Cain chose to disobey God, Cain's offspring wandered as homeless, spiritual orphans wreaking havoc among people wherever they went, and death was their consequence. All of it was displeasing in the sight of the Lord.

Throughout Scripture and throughout history, we have seen people choose lifestyles of sin instead of running to the presence of God. I know I lived a lifestyle of sinful choices before I finally understood who God was to me. Just as God extended grace to Noah and his family on the ark, God extends grace to all people today. Not just some people, but *all* people. Grace is the game-changer. Some people accept His grace, and some don't.

When we forget where we came from, we forget grace. God extended His grace to us in that while we were still sinners, Christ died for us (Rom. 5:8). God did *not have* to extend grace, but He chose to do it out of love. The stench of our sin is intolerable to a righteous and holy God. The only way to rescue us from the grave was for God to send His only Son to the grave in our place. Jesus went to a place you and I, believer, will never experience.

Let that sink in for a moment—Jesus endured hell so that you and I would never have to. He did that not only for you and me, but He did it even for those who deny

Him right at this very moment. They still have breath in their lungs to say, "Yes."

Jesus heard the eternal moans and groans of all those who never found reconciliation with God. That right there makes me weep. Jesus saw the faces of the people who rejected God, and they saw His. Jesus couldn't raise those dead from their graves. They were in their eternal grave. Don't let anybody on your watch spend their eternity in the place where Jesus isn't present.

Take a minute to remember the grace you received so you can lead others to the same source of this grace.

Can you imagine the jeers and stares Noah received as he put the ark together piece by piece? Even more, I wonder the emotions Noah and his family faced as they walked onto the ark. If what God said was really going to take place, I don't know about you, but my claustrophobiameter would have been on high alert. I also would be sad for all those I couldn't get on the ark. It makes me think whether I would really put my oxygen mask on first if they fell in the airplane cabin during an emergency or if I would struggle to make sure my children's masks were on first.

Scripture doesn't record Noah's concern about anyone. I often wonder why. Unlike Jonah, God didn't give any directives to Noah to warn people or give them an opportunity to repent. He told Noah to build the ark and then told Noah to take his family and get on the ark to save them. The ark would be the life-preserver to spare their lives, as well as the vessel from which God's chosen people would emerge after the waters receded. Something new was to be birthed.

When God closed the door of the ark on the day He designated (Gen. 7:16), God shut the door on that chapter of humanity. However righteous Noah was, not one of us is righteous, not one (Eccl. 7:20). Mercy is what got Noah on that boat. The closing of the ark door represented the salvific gift Jesus would eventually offer to the world through His sacrifice. On the cross, Jesus closed the door to our past and opened the door to our future. When the door on the ark finally opened, a whole new chapter unfolded.

Even though Noah and his family witnessed a miracle of God during those long days and nights of rain and darkness, once the land became dry and their new journey on land began, they struggled to do what was right. Some people can't shake what they've lived and seen. God said Noah was righteous but that doesn't mean his sons were all righteous. They all had lived in the sinful environment that offended God. They witnessed and experienced the debauchery that caused the earth to be flooded in the first place.

Most of us have always thought of Noah as righteous both before and after the flood. He obeyed God when God told him to build a big boat in the middle of the desert while all the people laughed and thought he was crazy. But the account in Genesis 9:21 causes me to pause for a moment. Why was Noah, a righteous man according to God, drinking so much wine (at six hundred years old!)

that he passed out naked in his tent? Had he done it before this recorded event? Was Ham the rebellious child or was he learning things from his dad? What was going on with Noah?

In Genesis 9:21–22, we read that after Noah drank too much wine and stumbled naked into his tent, his son Ham shamed the family by looking at his father's nakedness and going to tell his brothers, Shem and Japheth. Instead of repeating their brother's behavior, Shem and Japheth did what they were supposed to do and covered up their father.

When Noah woke up, he heard what Ham had done and delivered a curse upon Canaan, the son of Ham: "Cursed be Canaan! The lowest of slaves will he be to his brothers" (Gen. 9:25). Not only did Noah curse Canaan, but he blessed Shem and Japheth. I'm sure this didn't go over well at family gatherings!

> Praise be to the Lord, the God of Shem! May Canaan be the slave of Shem. May God extend Japheth's territory; may Japheth live in the tents of Shem, and may Canaan be the slave of Japheth.
> —GENESIS 9:26–27

Noah's descendants kept moving east (Gen. 11:2). Hopefully, you are noticing a trend by now: the farther we move from God, the easier it is to sin. At one time, everyone in the world spoke the same language, and people eventually settled in the land of Babylonia (Gen. 11:1–2). However, bad habits die hard and the sin of pride and rebellion once again rose up in the people. The people wanted to make themselves famous. Sounds very similar to the fame and power Lucifer wanted too. The people began to build a tower shooting straight up into the sky toward heaven.

God didn't choose someone to do the correcting this time. Instead, God went down from heaven with His angelic force, confused the people with different languages, and scattered them all over the world so they would not be able to continue in their self-reliance (Gen. 11:7–8). The people whom God spared from complete destruction fell into a lifestyle of sin and estrangement from God just as all the others had before them.

But God.

God had another solution for these wayward people. He was about to call a spiritual father for these spiritual orphans. His name was Abram.

Advocating for the Spiritual Orphan

1. How often do you reflect on the grace God has extended to you? Remembering our past is not an exercise in bringing up old shame or regret but rather an exercise in breathing in the goodness of God.

2. Do you withhold grace from others because of their sin? Do you have a hard time reaching out to those whom you believe deserve judgment instead of grace?

3. Have you ever thought of a person as a spiritual orphan before? How does seeing the person as an orphan rather than a sinner change your lens?

4. What are some of the ways God is calling you to reach out to people who are spiritual orphans? How does God put you into situations to help the lost?

5. How can you encourage people to move closer to God instead of running from Him?

Chapter Two

FAMILY BAGGAGE

BRAM WAS FROM the lineage of Noah's son, Shem. He was the son of Terah. Abram lived in a land full of people doing life far from God. However, God was about to move Abram and set him on the path to his purpose.

We don't know much about Abram, but we know his family was into idol worship. As people moved farther from the presence of God, their need for new gods increased because if God wasn't their priority, they were going to seek assistance from something or someone other than God in order to meet their needs. God knew Abram would be distracted and quite possibly discouraged by the culture he lived in so God told Abram to move.

> The LORD had said to Abram, "Go from your country, your people and your father's household to the land I will show you."
>
> —GENESIS 12:1

God chose this one man, Abram, to be the father of many nations. The spiritual tone Abram set would affect future generations of God's chosen people, including you and me. Would it be possible for one man and one woman to parent these ungodly people? Apart from God, no. With God, anything is possible.

Abram wasn't perfect, but God is a God of covenant. Just as with Noah, God kept His covenant despite the fact that His people always returned to sin. God told Abram that nations would be born from him, and that is exactly what happened. Were the nations perfect? Unfortunately, no. What could have possibly made the outcome different? Multiplication.

There is power in multiplication. One becomes two, two becomes eight, eight becomes sixteen, and so on. Father Abraham couldn't do it all by himself. He needed others who would also make the decision to do what was right in the sight of the Lord. Their right living would become an example to others to live rightly. If sin can be duplicated so too can right living. We need more people today who will live right so that others may see right living modeled.

Do you ever have self-righteous conversations with your Bible when you are reading it? I hope I'm not the only one! Sometimes I find myself saying things like, "Good grief. What will it take to convince you people to do the right thing?" or "How could you miss it? You saw the glory of God on the mountain and yet, you were down below wrapped in sin. What is wrong with you people?"

It's in those moments when I think or utter these words that a spirit of conviction and grief well up in my heart. I was that person who couldn't get it right. We are that people. We live out our days under the shadow of the Cross and the rolled-away stone. We are no better than those who tossed their jewelry into the fire and worshiped the golden calf that emerged from the fire. (See Exodus 32.)

I can only imagine how Moses must have felt when he threw down the stone tablets during his holy temper tantrum.

> When Moses approached the camp and saw the calf and the dancing, his anger burned and he threw the tablets out of his hands, breaking them to pieces at the foot of the mountain.
> —EXODUS 32:19

Why was Moses so angry? Because before Moses went down from the mountain, he pleaded with God on the people's behalf (Exod. 32:11–14). He begged God not to destroy the people.

If we pray, we pray for people to change. But, like Moses, the minute we see no change has taken place, we get angry, frustrated, and sometimes we even throw temper tantrums. We withhold grace and instead replace it with judgment. What right do we have to do this? Absolutely none. God gets to choose whom He wants to spare and forgive. He's the only one righteous enough to fulfill this role. All God asks us to do is to tell the world about Jesus and allow the Holy Spirit to do the rest. Our sinfulness and need for a Savior should always be at the forefront of our mind. Otherwise, if we forget where we came from, we run into the quicksand of becoming self-righteous like the Pharisees and grace-less.

How can we care for the spiritual orphan who is without

their Father if we look at them in disgust and disdain? Lost people need advocates not adversaries. Jesus, on the Cross, said, "Father, forgive them, for they do not know what they are doing" (Luke 23:34).

The spiritual orphan knows nothing about grace, faith, and obedience because they don't know their Father. It's our job to show them who He is. We do this by extending love and grace to all. George Whitefield, the great evangelist of the Second Great Awakening said, "When you hear of a notorious sinner, instead of thinking you do well to be angry, beg of Jesus Christ to convert, and make him a monument of his free grace."[9]

Far too often, we enable Satan to do greater works in the lost by our attitude toward the lost. I looked up the definition for *adversary*. Guess whose name was in there? The devil's. The Bible says the devil is our adversary and he is out to destroy us (1 Pet. 5:8). If we aren't building up and encouraging people, we are acting more like little Satans than little Christs.

Two years ago, I became acquainted with a ministry called Outcry in the Barrio located just a few miles south of where I lived. The Outcry is a group home that welcomes in men battling addictions. No one is forced to go, and no one is forced to stay. In the home, they are expected to abide by the house rules, and whether a person cares to or not, every person there will hear about Jesus.

Freddie and Ninfa Garcia, the founders of this ministry, grew up impoverished in San Antonio, Texas. Like many youth in his neighborhood, Freddie turned to gangs, violence, robbery, and drugs. During his younger years, he was not someone you would have wanted to encounter on the street. Eventually, his drug problem ruled over him. He was in and out of jail, had children out of wedlock, and was dangerously close to losing his life to drugs.

Until Jesus.

Through different connections, Freddie found himself in Los Angeles with a person who, at one time, sold drugs in Freddie's neighborhood. This friend shared with Freddie the hope of Jesus Christ. Freddie needed hope because his life was a living hell. However, Freddie's hard heart initially caused him not to want to hear anything about Jesus. But by one former drug addict simply loving Freddie through his mess, Freddie eventually gave his life to Jesus and immediately, everything changed for him. He was no longer plagued by addiction, and his heart burst with love for people—all people.

In his book, *Outcry in the Barrio*[10], Freddie shares about how much he hated white people because of his Mexican heritage. However, as soon as Jesus became Lord of Freddie's life, the hate went away. Shortly after becoming a Christian, he knew he was called to return to his stomping grounds to reach the drug dealers and addicts in his old neighborhood and deliver the same hope Jesus gives freely to all who believe.

Freddie and Ninfa eventually returned to San Antonio and slowly over time, their ministry, Victory Outreach, was started. As Freddie went out on the streets to hand out tracts to the drug dealers, addicts began to show up at his house and asked for Freddie's help to kick their addiction. Freddie and Ninfa allowed these men, and sometimes women, to move into their small home and do life with their young family. At one point, there were so many people living at the house that some of them slept in junked-out cars in the Garcia's back yard.

The Garcias' ministry birthed ministry homes in many cities across the United States and overseas. These group homes have also birthed churches to serve their communities.

Freddie Garcia was on a destructive path, but Jesus plucked him from death and raised him to life. Freddie could have stopped right there, but he didn't. He wanted to give back what he had been given because he knew the brokenness addiction caused. He hurt his relationships with family, relationships with his children, and hurt his health because of his addiction. He knew there was a way for people who wanted to be made whole to find healing in the name of Jesus, and if he didn't reach those held in the bondage of addiction, who would?

> *What causes division, strife, and misery among men is not race, culture, language, or class but sin and rebellion.*[11]
> —FREDDIE GARCIA

Jesus healed Freddie's heart and saved his life, and because of Freddie and Ninfa's obedience, many have found not only healing from addiction, but they have also found life in Christ. Many of these men and women were without physical parents for various reasons, but Freddie and Ninfa became spiritual parents to these lost and orphaned souls. They discipled each person and asked them to do the same. They were not interested in giving handouts or temporary fixes. They were building a godly army of soldiers—both men and women—to battle the darkness that is addiction. Freddie and Ninfa diligently taught their spiritual sons the Word of God and fed them, clothed them, and housed them.

At one point several years in, the ministry was growing and people had been launched out to various locations. Freddie knew it was time to give independence to his spiritual sons, so he held a meeting with the men one night. He let them know it was time for them to fly independently of Freddie. They were ready, he said. He also needed to let them go so that he could work with their "younger brothers." The men, however, felt as though Freddie was acting like every other person in their life. They thought Freddie was trying to get rid of them. They didn't see that becoming independent was a sign of success and obedience. Freddie assured the men they were family, they would always be family, and the thing that held them together was their love for each other in Christ. Freddie said, "I'm still your spiritual father."

I love the Garcias' story for so many reasons. Instead of pursuing the American dream after they were delivered from addiction, they went after those who were living a nightmare. How many of you reading this would intentionally choose to actively engage drug dealers and other criminals with the gospel? How many of you would allow addicts not only into your home for dinner, but would also move your small children into your bedroom because you've given up all the other rooms as dorms?

The Garcias' ministry continues today through their children. Their children could have been lost to the streets, crime, and addiction, but because of the life Freddie and Ninfa modeled, their adult children are now carrying on the ministry and continuing to reach every single person— rich, poor, white, black, brown, addict, adulterer—whose soul is in need of the Savior. Their youngest son is the lead pastor for their church, and he ministers continually to his neighbors and all those who come to his door.

People don't always believe the truth about God's love because they haven't had a rock-bottom encounter with Jesus. Regardless of the circumstances of the encounter, they haven't recognized their own spiritual depravity or need for a Savior. Not everyone who cries out to the Father in Jesus's name has a physical problem, but every single person who has this moment has a spiritual problem before they say yes to Jesus. Many people will be deceitfully led to believe that their faith is linked to church membership or the faith (or lack thereof) of their parents. The problem with that is far too many people don't personally believe because they haven't personally pursued Jesus. Maybe they've heard about Jesus or said a prayer as a child, but that's where it all ended. They walk through life spiritually dry and completely unable to care for themselves let alone the orphan, the lame, and the poor because they aren't filled with the things of the Spirit.

God wants us to do far more than just hear about Jesus and be saved; He wants us to be Jesus's hands and feet in this world. (See 1 Corinthians 12:27.) If you are a parent, you know that parenting doesn't turn off, it doesn't take vacations, it doesn't matter if you haven't been fed, and it certainly isn't always pretty. But would most of us abandon our children for easy living? I don't think so. If we say these dangerous words, "Send me, Lord!" we must be prepared to go anywhere and do anything the Spirit asks of us.

———

For the Israelites, family lineage meant everything. Who you were determined what you did and where you lived. Family was important. The parents of the home were commanded to raise their children in the right way so they would know the Lord, know His commands, and not depart from His path for their lives. God had warned the Israelites time and again not to marry foreigners because God knew they worshipped other gods. God told the Israelites not to have any other gods except Him (Exod. 20:3). If a parent failed to set a good example or make sure a child understood what the dire consequences of failing to obey God could be, it didn't end well (Exod. 20:5). As many of us know, sometimes children listen and sometimes they don't. It's all part of living in a broken world.

During the turbulent, violent, and momentous events in Israel's period of the judges, a story of ordinary life is relayed to us in the account known as the Book of Ruth. During this time period, virtually every family depended on their own crops and livestock for food and their necessities. When drought and famine came to the place we know as Bethlehem, a father seeking food for his family moved his family to Moab. The father, Elimelech, who was married to Naomi made the mistake of entering into the foreign lands God said not to enter. Instead of trusting God for provision in Bethlehem, Elimelech relied on his own strength and decisions. While in the land of Moab, Elimelech's two sons married Moabite women. These Moabite women worshipped their own gods. In the land where Elimelech sought provision for his family, death occurred instead. Elimelech and both of his sons died in Moab leaving his wife and two daughters-in-law to provide for themselves.

Naomi, hearing that the famine was over in Bethlehem, made plans to return home. Naomi took both daughters-in-law on the journey, however, somewhere along the road, she told them both they could return home to their mothers (Ruth 1:6–8). Although they both initially protested and said they both wanted to stay with Naomi, Orpah returned home. Ruth stayed with Naomi. Right there on a dusty road to Bethlehem, Ruth professed her faith in a God she had not yet claimed as her own.

> But Ruth replied, "Don't urge me to leave you or to turn back from you. Where you go I will go, and where you stay I will stay. Your people will be my people and your God my God. Where you die I will die, and there I will be buried. May the LORD deal with me, be it ever so severely, if even death separates you and me.
>
> —RUTH 1:16–17

You know what jumps out to me more than anything in this story? The love Naomi had for Ruth. Naomi was a God-fearing Israelite woman, yet she loved her pagan daughter-in-law and cared for her as her own. In verse fourteen of the first chapter of Ruth, it says "Ruth clung tightly to Naomi." How tightly are pagans clinging to you? Even Orpah who made the decision to return to her mother, kissed Naomi before she left. Naomi cared for these women even as she needed to be cared for herself. This encounter makes me think of a story Bob Goff shared in his book *Everybody Always*.[12]

Bob arrived for an event in Florida and unbeknownst to him, the event coordinators arranged for a limousine to pick him up. Because he didn't want to waste their money, he obliged and got into the limousine. He quickly struck up a conversation with the limo driver. Realizing the driver was almost ready to retire, Bob asked him if he had ever been in the back of a limo. The driver's response was, "Of course not. I'd be fired." Convincing the driver that it didn't matter anyway since he was about to retire, they pulled over and Bob got in the front and the driver got into the back of the limo.

When they arrived at Bob's destination, Bob opened the back door and let his new friend out, gave him a hug, and sent him off with some affirming words. This doesn't seem too far out there, right? I mean, it sounds like great fun. However, it was Bob's next sentence that made me stop and think for a minute:

When the limo driver went home that night to the woman he'd been living with for the past ten years, do you think he told her he'd met a Christian guy that day who told him he was supposed to be married? Of course not! I bet he told her he'd met a guy who told him who he was.

The difference between Bob's conversation with the limo driver and what some Christian's conversations might have been is that Bob didn't point out this guy's sin; he simply had a conversation with him and built him up. The limo driver knew Bob was a Christian through their conversation. Sometimes we need to realize that if we allow the Holy Spirit to work through us, the things we say are exactly what Jesus needs us to say that day—and it isn't always the Sunday school answers we have memorized during evangelism training. We don't always need a scripted conversation planned in our head.

Sharing the gospel is super important for sure, but we also must realize we don't know what is going on in everyone's lives. Maybe they've had a conversation with God that day. Perhaps they are searching. Maybe they are even looking for the negative Christian to affirm their anger toward God and Christians. What matters is that we show love to everybody always and allow the Spirit to lead us in all things—even if it doesn't look exactly like we had planned for that moment. Anyone who has ever experienced awkwardly sharing the gospel for the sake of solely sharing the gospel knows it doesn't always turn out well (if you have ever done door-to-door evangelism you know exactly what I am talking about). We walk away rejected because the person didn't receive *our*—I mean, *the* gospel—message.

We shouldn't ever stop having gospel conversations, but some of us need to soften our message. We need to engage people better before we start sharing so they know we care. I so wish I could remember where I read this statement, but it said something along the lines of, "So many people invite us to church, but no one has invited us into their home." This statement was in response to transplants moving from one state to a Bible-belt state.

Shortly after I read this article, I had a conversation with a friend of mine about an idea I had. I mentioned this statement and she said, "Yes, it is like we are telling people there is something wrong with them before we even know them. We are telling them they need to go to church."

Don't get me wrong, church is the best place to be and a great place to be in community, but the push to get people into church, in many instances, is based on the ethnicity or lifestyle of people moving into an area. We are throwing out blanket assumptions that, because they are Indians, Asians, or Middle Eastern, they need to be in church so they can be saved.

Sometimes, we target those moving into a new area because of the state they came from. Often, we skip asking anything about their religious beliefs, where they worship, who they worship, and go straight to the invitation of, "Come to my church with me."

I know. I've done this. Many times, our churches talk about missions, but our pews look anything but missional.

Have you ever been in an uncomfortable situation? You know, the kind where you know people are staring and whispering and well, who knows what else? Me too. And so did Jesus.

> When one of the Pharisees invited Jesus to have dinner with him, he went to the Pharisee's house and reclined at the table. A woman in that town who lived a sinful life learned that Jesus was eating at the Pharisee's house, so she came there with an alabaster jar of perfume.
>
> As she stood behind him at his feet weeping, she began to wet his feet with her tears. Then she wiped them with her hair, kissed them and poured perfume on them.
>
> When the Pharisee who had invited him saw this, he said to himself, "If this man were a prophet, he would know who is touching him and what kind of woman she is—that she is a sinner."
>
> Jesus answered him, "Simon, I have something to tell you. Tell me, teacher, Two people owed money to a certain moneylender. One owed him five hundred denarii, and the other fifty. Neither of them had the money to pay him back, so he forgave the debts of both. Now which of them will love him more?"
>
> Simon replied, "I suppose the one who had the bigger debt forgiven."
>
> "You have judged correctly," Jesus said.
>
> Then he turned toward the woman and said to Simon, "Do you see this woman? I came into your house. You did not give me any water for my feet,

but she wet my feet with her tears and wiped them with her hair. You did not give me a kiss, but this woman, from the time I entered, has not stopped kissing my feet. You did not put oil on my head, but she has poured perfume on my feet. Therefore, I tell you, her many sins have been forgiven—as her great love has shown. But whoever has been forgiven little loves little."

Then Jesus said to her, "Your sins are forgiven."

The other guests began to say among themselves, "Who is this who even forgives sins?"

Jesus said to the woman, "Your faith has saved you; go in peace."

—LUKE 7:36–50

When I picture this account in my head, I picture total silence, as if you could hear a pin drop in that room. What may have been seconds, probably felt like hours to those who witnessed what took place. You know who probably didn't feel one bit uncomfortable, shocked, annoyed, bothered or anxious? Jesus.

I wish I could always say the same thing about myself, but I can't. Several years ago, I had to fight back my flesh. I had to fight the urge to care what others thought and take the focus off myself and put it on the Cross. Why? Because none of it had anything to do with me. If my purpose is to glorify God and to love others, I must be willing to lay down anything and everything that could get in the way of that. This includes my pride, conveniences, "me" time, and fear of what others may think.

Let me fill you in a little. One day, my husband and I

took our youngest two children to our neighborhood park. While my husband played tennis with my son, I took my daughter to the playground. As we parked our bikes near the playground, I noticed a man standing alone smoking a cigarette. I thought it was kind of odd. A few minutes later, the man approached me and asked me a question about a road. I gave him a quick answer. He left and walked toward a woman and a child. A short while later, I glanced over to the tennis courts and noticed that this same man was playing tennis with my husband and son as his wife and young son watched.

Because I am nosey, I coerced my daughter into finishing up her playground time so that we could make our way over to the tennis courts. In a matter of minutes, I learned that our new friend had recently moved from Iraq. It's a long story of how he got here. Their story is not unusual, and I've since learned that this happens frequently, especially for those who help Americans in Iraq. My husband gave our new friend his cell phone number, and we all left.

My husband met with our new friend a couple times and chatted via text messages. After about a month or so, my husband told me that our new friends asked to meet us at our church. Our new friend and one of his other Iraqi friends came the first time. Our new friends were Muslim. One had been in a Christian church before. The other never had. Since they spoke English, they could follow along. It went well, and they said they would like to return.

They came to church again the following week. That

time, our friend's wife and young child came with them. I met them to get their son registered for childcare. I was so thankful the husband spoke English because his wife spoke hardly any. We got their son settled into his childcare room and he, without hesitation, went right in. My kids never went right into childcare as young children, especially in a strange place, so I took that as a good sign. He thought he was at Chuck E. Cheese because of all the painted murals on the walls in the children's ministry building. Honestly, that is the one and *only* time I've ever been thankful for Chuck E. Cheese.

Because our new friends were from Iraq and because they were Muslim, the wife wore a hijab (for those of you who do not know what that is, it is a head covering). Of course, I knew she would be wearing one, but I didn't really think anything of it until they arrived in our church atrium. It was then that I realized the whiteness of our church. I knew then and there that it was not going to be an ordinary church service. This wasn't our first time bringing a Muslim to church, but it was the first time I was with someone in our church wearing a hijab.

I took a deep breath, and we went into the worship center. Even though I was trying to breathe normally, I noticed my breathing became more shallow. My husband hadn't yet come down to meet us, so I was walking them in all by myself. There was no way we could just blend in with the crowd and sit toward the back because my family always sat on the second row of our gigantic worship center. Not only were we walking into unchartered territory, we were placing this family and their friend front and center. And because no one sat in front of us, it felt like all eyes were on us.

The worship set finally began. Everyone stood except for the three guests with us. The songs seemed endless. When the greeting came, they stood (praise God!) and greeted people. After we sat down, our friend leaned over and said, "After prayers in the mosque, we do the greeting too." And then, more worship. And again, they did not stand up. I was trying my best to engage in worship and block it all out, but I was struggling.

After the worship, we sat and the message began. I thought that would be my safe zone, but I totally spaced out on the fact that the wife did not speak English. At times, the husband felt compelled to translate for her (yes, out loud in case you are wondering). It was a great message, and I was grateful we were in a sermon series on the Ten Commandments because Muslims understand those.

But let me tell you, I prayed through the whole service, "Lord, help me fight back the fear, the insecurity right now. I know people are looking (I see them glancing) every time our friend translates (you know, like when people have a screaming child in church kind of staring). I see them shifting in their seats. Where is my quiet time? This is *my* time to hear from you. Lord, forgive me for being selfish. This isn't about me. This is about them. This is about You. You have them here for a reason. May I not get in their way nor may anyone else here for that matter. Amen."

This prayer went on and on in my head during the

entire message. By the end, I was exhausted and my neck and back hurt from being so tense.

However, there was a glimmer of hope. Our church does an invitation, and after we pray, everyone stands. Our friend stood during the invitation time (no, I do not think he was responding to the invitation, but he was engaging at least). They also went to our Bible fellowship class after service, heard the gospel again, and learned about some verses from Ephesians (specifically about grace and peace—God's timing). We spent time with them after class with some other class members getting frozen yogurt.

A couple days after church, I got the privilege of taking the wife to the doctor for her prenatal appointment. They allowed me to take her because the husband works during the day. What a privilege and honor it was that they trusted me so quickly. It was a miracle from God that I found a doctor that would see her, and that the doctor allowed me into the examination room. Because of the language barrier, I relied on a translator app. There were a lot of laughs that day because as good as apps are, things get lost in translation. I learned that day that she was a young girl of nineteen and was already the mother of a three-year-old. Her husband was almost twice her age. I texted a friend after the appointment and said that this girl must just be completely overwhelmed.

I knew she was younger, but it was really hard to tell with her hijab on, and I hadn't had a good chance to study her face. Eye contact was not her strong suit perhaps because of her culture. She had a healthy baby girl a few months after this appointment, and they asked me to visit them in the hospital. Without her hijab on, I saw her beautiful long hair and her youth.

She went back to Iraq with her daughter a couple years after this encounter, and I still hear from her husband from time to time. They never professed Jesus as their Savior that I know of, but I know that my family was part of planting a seed. I pray often that there is someone watering that seed to this day.

A missionary friend posted in his missions update once that "the kingdom of God advances best through friendships and it is going to take everyone who has the Spirit of God...to invest in friendships with people that are culturally and religiously different." Even if it means being uncomfortable among your own people.

Be a part of changing lives. Remember that moment when you first received and understood the good news? I do. Now, help someone else hear that good news too.

> This same Good News that came to you is going out all over the world. It is bearing fruit everywhere by changing lives, just as it changed your lives from the day you first heard and understood the truth about God's wonderful grace.
>
> —COLOSSIANS 1:6, NLT

Live and love. We can preach the gospel, but we also need to love others just as Jesus loved the woman with the alabaster jar. We need to stop looking at everyone who is not a Christian through Pharisaical eyes. If Jesus loved the woman with the alabaster jar, we must too. If Jesus endured stares from the crowd, we will too. Jesus did it for His Father, and we must too.

Spiritual orphans need love and nurturing. They must know we care about them. Naomi cared for her daughters-in-law. Jesus told us to feed His sheep. A lot of the sheep don't yet know Jesus as their Shepherd, and it is our job to help them know about Him. The call is to care enough to care—and care we must.

Advocating for the Spiritual Orphan

1. Who are the spiritual orphans God has placed in your life? Are they in your family or in your sphere of influence? Name them by name so they become as real to you as they are to God.

2. Do you sometimes think God has called other people to reach the lost in big ways but you've not been given the call? Do you feel you are not called or qualified? What would it mean to you to be called or qualified?

3. Do you think only people who make radical sacrifices like the Garcias accomplish great works for the kingdom? Why or why not?

4. How important do you think spiritual mentors are in people's lives?

5. Do you have margin in your life to become a spiritual mentor? Why or why not?

Chapter Three

THE CALL

T HE HEART IS the wellspring of life both literally and figuratively. When our heart stops beating, we die physically. When our heart stops beating spiritually, we also die. Both deaths result in a ripple effect on those around us.

> Above all else, guard your heart, for it is the wellspring of life.
> —PROVERBS 4:23

What this country, and more importantly Christians, need most is a heart revival. Our hearts need to be revived to love God and to love others. Christians relying on their strength first and God second is rampant. Christians acting unloving to others is also rampant. We speak "love" (sometimes) from our mouths, but our hearts are not in line with how we act and think. God knows, and other people know too (Matt. 12:34).

Whether we care to admit it or not, our sinful nature can spring up at any moment if we are not careful. When we are spiritually empty, exhausted, or complacent, we make room for more of ourselves than for the Holy Spirit.

Ever find yourself rushing down the sidewalk to meet someone for coffee or lunch only to find yourself a little put out by the dirty, smelly, and maybe even intimidating homeless person taking up residence in your path? Assuming you are not staring down at your phone or engaged in a phone call during your sprint, what is the first thing your heart says when you see that person? Is it, "Here's another one." Or maybe, "Why don't they just a get a job for goodness sakes?" How about, "I'd love to give them a few dollars, but they are probably going to use it to buy drugs or alcohol anyway." All those thoughts may be valid, but how often do you acknowledge him or her with a smile, eye contact or a, "How are you doing?" No greater conviction comes than when you hear your children saying the things your ugly heart mutters under its breath.

> The Fathers of the Church were not afraid to go out into the desert because they had a richness in their hearts. But we, with richness all around us, are afraid, because the desert is in our hearts.[13]
>
> — FRANK KAFKA

If words speak death or life (Prov. 18:21), we need to work on being better speakers of life. And often, our actions speak louder than words do. Jesus said that if we took care of the least, we were actually taking care of Him. (See Matthew 25:35–40.) It doesn't take much to figure out what the opposite of what He said is.

I believe we need a heart revival in the Christian world before we can do a better job of reaching the world. God knows our heart even more than we know our heart. He knows what we think before we speak or act (Ps. 139:2).

———————————

Christian worship artist Lauren Daigle has taken the music charts by storm. Her albums are crossing the bridge from Christian music to pop music. Her first album, *How Can It Be,* went platinum and her second album, *Look Up Child,* is stirring up the music world. Her chart history caught the talk shows' interest and Lauren found herself appearing on both the *Ellen* show and *Late Night with Jimmy Fallon.* Both times, she sang songs from her *Look Up Child* album, and both times she received criticism from some Christians because she didn't overtly speak the name of God. Here's a young woman who writes and sings soulfully deep lyrics of worship to her Father and shares them with the world. This gift wasn't something she created on her own; it was a gift placed in her by the Creator.

Some Christians also blasted her because she appeared on Ellen's show claiming Lauren should never have appeared on the show because Ellen is openly homosexual. In response to the criticism, Lauren said, "I think the second we start drawing lines around which people are able to be approached and which aren't, we've already completely missed the heart of God."[14] Being wise about the company we keep and the things we do and watch is one thing, but withdrawing ourselves from the opportunities God places in our lives only demonstrates that some have forgotten the call of God. The call is to go out and be light in the dark world. God knows how bad it is, but

He also promises us He is with us and that we are not to be afraid.

There are Christians today doing a better job at tearing down the witness for the gospel than those who claim to not believe in God at all. Jesus had a name for these people who act like this. He called them hypocrites. Merriam-Webster defines a *hypocrite* as "a person who puts on a false appearance of virtue or religion and a person who acts in contradiction to his or her stated beliefs or feelings."[15]

When we say God is love, that Christians are made in the image of God, and that New Testament believers are filled with the Holy Spirit (whose fruit includes love), but we aren't acting like love, we are hypocrites. It is plain and simple. It may sting a little to hear these words, but correction isn't always pain-free. If your heart is reacting to these words right now, a spirit of conviction may be at work.

I desperately want to be the person who loves everyone without hesitation or judgment. It is a real struggle, if I am completely honest, to think like Jesus first. When I see someone who looks different than me, what is my first thought? Is it Jesus filtered first and foremost? Instead of judging outward appearances or actions, I want to be like Christ who goes straight to the condition of a person's heart. And you know what? You and I can be like this because we have the Holy Spirit within us. When we rely on the strength and the power of the Holy Spirit in us, we gain wisdom, discernment, empathy, and love that our human hearts can't muster on their own.

God needs to transform our hearts radically. Far too many are wavering in lukewarm waters toward God and others, and we are creating collateral damage for His bride. When nonbelievers act kinder and more moral than those who claim to be Christians, it hinders the potential to reach that person with the gospel because, to them, why would they want to become unkind, unloving, and less moral in order to become a Christian?

At the opposite end of the spectrum, if someone is acting foolish and living a life riddled with sin and ungodliness, and they see a Christian partaking of the same foolishness and sin, why would they think they need to do anything different? It's hard to speak about eternity when we are earthly minded people unless the goodness of eternity has overwhelmed and wrecked us so thoroughly that we can't help but to live like Christ and for Christ.

At your annual exam, or anytime you visit a doctor for that matter, the doctor always listens to your heart because what's going on in your heart helps them understand what might be going on with the rest of your body. It is the same spiritually. If we are willing to let God exam our hearts, what would He find? Even if you think your heart is in great shape, it still needs to be exercised and trained. There is always work to do in our hearts.

To *revive* something means "to restore from a depressed, inactive, or unused state."[16] We as a people need God to revive our hearts again toward loving Him and others. We need to replace the deserts within our hearts with flourishing gardens of fruit and fields ripe with harvest. But He needs us to want to. If a person revives an old, antique car to its original state but never takes it for a spin outside of its garage, the revitalization is for naught. The vehicle might work and have potential, but it will never get the opportunity to be used for its purpose.

Friend, we need God to revive our hearts. We need to beg Him to revive our hearts so that the stuff of ourselves will flush out and make room for the Holy Spirit to overflow within us. We need to want to be pure vessels for Christ to reach those who need to know their Father. The drowning who cannot call for help need to be our heart's focus.

May the Potter's hands perform a work so great throughout the church that a spiritual marker is set that will produce a massive generational heart revival not only among non-Christians but also among those claiming to be Christians. It's been done before, and it can be done again. It only takes one.

On a dry, dusty, and ordinary afternoon, Jesus led the disciples straight into territory no Jewish person wanted to venture into. Jesus had a purpose for the detour when He and the disciples arrived at Jacob's Well in Sychar. They were all hot, thirsty, and hungry. Jesus sent the disciples into a local town to find food, but he stayed at the well. It was at this well that a Samaritan woman arrived in the heat of the day to fill her water jar. She was not regarded highly by the people in her village, but Jesus didn't feel the same way about her. He went out of His way that day to show love toward this woman.

Jesus knew this woman wanted and needed so much more than another man, friends, an easy life, or water. He knew she needed God's love and peace. After this radical encounter with Jesus at the well, this woman discovered and accepted the living water she was desperately looking for. She didn't keep this encounter or her Savior to herself. Scripture says she left her water jar—the thing she went to the well to fill—and ran home (about a mile and a half) to tell the people what Jesus had said (John 4:28–29) and who He is. The Bible says, "Many of the Samaritans from that town believed in him because of the woman's testimony" (John 4:39).

For some, all it took was her testimony and her change of countenance. You see, before her encounter with Jesus, she was a loner, a shunned woman in her community who didn't even feel worthy enough to draw water with the other women. But after her encounter, she was joyful, she admitted her wrong doing (repentance and confession), and she wanted everyone else to know and experience Jesus (her testimony).

However, not everyone believed right away. Some were still hard-hearted. Either they didn't believe Jesus was the Savior, or they couldn't separate the woman from her sin. They asked Jesus to stay a few more days, and a few days with Jesus was all it took. More people encountered the Messiah through the words Jesus spoke. The people said to the woman, "We no longer believe just because of what you said; now we have heard for ourselves, and we know that this man really is the Savior of the world" (John 4:42).

There is much to be thankful for in this account. Because

of one woman, so many people personally believed in Jesus as their Savior. I've read this passage and written on this passage so many times, but as I read it this time in this context, something stood out to me. What if Jesus hadn't stayed a few more days? How many people might not have ever believed in Jesus because their hearts were so hardened toward this woman? Instead of reflecting on their own sinful attitudes, they were staring down her sin and not loving her well. Jesus was gracious to say yes to staying a few more days, but we don't always get that extra opportunity.

I had my own village moment once. I wasn't the woman at the well (at least in the example I'm about to give), but I was one of those who did the shunning and the judging. I discovered my step-dad was addicted to a hard-core drug during my junior year of high school. I was the opposite of loving toward him and the whole situation. I was angry—teenage girl kind of angry. I was pouty, and my poutiness turned to rebellion. It was not one of my finer moments, and my hateful attitude thrust me into some dangerous behavior.

I didn't know Christ at the time, and in fact, this revelation made my heart hard toward church. My parents attended church every week and took us along, but I couldn't rationalize the behavior with his faith. I had no sympathy and no empathy for him. I was angry he had hurt my mom in this way, and because I was teenage-angry, I blamed our family problems on him and his lack of leading us well. I was so empty, and emptiness makes it impossible to love. Hurt people hurt people. We are only able to love out of our overflow. If we aren't filled up with His love, we most certainly won't love all people. There will always be a condition or limit to our love.

Shortly after finding out my stepdad was doing drugs, I vaguely remember attending an addiction-recovery church service. It wasn't anything like the church services I attended growing up. There was so much freedom in that service. People raised their hands during worship. Looking back, I wish my heart had been softer at the time because my life for the next several years might have looked a lot different had I encountered the living Christ during that service instead of withholding grace from my stepdad and being filled with so much anger. I knew my step-dad had a tough upbringing with his own father. I knew he was a Vietnam veteran, battling who knows what else. Still, I saw him through my eyes instead of seeing him the way Jesus saw him at the lowest point of his addiction. He was a child in need of adoption by the Father. I don't know if he accepted Christ then. We never talked about it. He needed people who would walk alongside him and pour wisdom into him. As far as I could tell, either no one stepped in to do that or he was not in a place yet where he wanted to follow Jesus because he continued to make bad choices and I continued to spiral.

Although my grace-less behavior was from when I was a nonbeliever, I must admit I've had these same feelings for some people as a believer. If I've been hurt by them, I can easily form my own opinion about them. If I don't agree with their choices or lifestyle, I might not be interested in sacrificing my time to deal with the messy parts of doing life with a person who may not be like me. I know I am not the only one who does this or feels this way. That's why the image of seeing someone as a spiritual orphan has opened my eyes (thank you, Holy Spirit), and I hope it is opening your eyes as well. I wouldn't walk past an orphan child sitting all alone on the side of a road so why would I do the same to someone who is a spiritual orphan? Why would any of us?

I recently learned the woman at the well's name. In her book *Without Rival*, Lisa Bevere found through her research that the woman's name was Photina.[17] Photina not only played a huge part in introducing her village to Jesus, but Photina was also present on the day of Pentecost and received the same Holy Spirit all those who were present received. The Holy Spirit—as He did with Peter, John, and many others since then—gave her even more boldness to preach the good news. She went on to preach in many towns from Carthage in northern Africa all the way to Rome. In Rome, she boldly told the Emperor Nero about his need for Jesus. She, along with her five sisters and two sons were martyrs for the cause of Christ.

Because people in Photina's village knew everything about her, they didn't desire to spend time with her or show her love or compassion. We don't even know if the man she was living with at the time loved her. But Jesus loved Photina, and He intentionally pursued her. It was up to her to say yes or no to the Savior that hot afternoon at Jacob's Well. She allowed others to keep her from community. Who knows if any of her husbands had died? Maybe she was a poor widow who kept being taken in by men. Perhaps this last man was using her as a slave. We don't know for sure. But we do know that people didn't want to be around her. She was sad, lonely, and desperate. She found—and lost—her identity in men, and she didn't find her complete identity until she found Jesus. Jesus was the only one who could meet her deepest need. This need wasn't the physical water she was desiring. It was a spiritual need for the living water which fills us and satisfies us for all eternity.

Like her, many today wander through life without feeling loved. They've been hurt and let down by so many people in their lives. Their ability to trust and feel worthy is gone. So, they wallow in sadness desperate for someone to acknowledge them. And usually, they cling to the first person that comes along who shows them love, even if that love isn't well-intentioned. Many continue in a pattern of abuse, addiction, and depression. Photina knew about God, but she didn't personally know her Father. It took an encounter with Jesus to change her perspective.

The spiritual orphan is no different. People desperately want someone to care for them and provide for them in a way no earthly person can. It's a hole in our heart God formed when He made each one of us. Before a spiritual orphan knows the One who loves them more than they can imagine, they might only find themselves running to God or some form of a god when they have a need or are at their lowest point. Our physical needs are so less important than the spiritual need only God the Father can meet. Sometimes we lose valuable years snubbing God. And, most will suffer consequences for disobeying God. What if you, I, and the church at large would be more focused on being proactive instead of reactive when it comes to spiritual orphans? What if we loved the hardest people better? If we did, I guarantee it would change the world.

A dear friend who I have had the privilege to know for the past few years answered the call to care for street orphans in the Philippines. After a mission trip during high school, Natalie could not shake the feeling of needing to do something for the orphans. After a series of God-orchestrated opportunities she outlines in her book, *The Forgotten Ones*,[18] Natalie found herself living and serving full-time in the Philippines. She had to learn the local dialect and customs. She found herself drawn to the street children of Mynaw.

Street children in Mynaw, as in places in other parts of the world, are the invisible children. They literally sleep on the streets and care for themselves. They often take to stealing to survive, become addicted to drugs, and are targets for trafficking. They live and sleep wherever they can find a place and are constantly at risk. You can imagine how hardened they must be simply to survive.

Natalie's ministry was simple: serve the street orphans. Every day, she and her spiritual sister, Brin, would go to where the street children hung out in the city center. She would engage them with conversation. As a blonde, white young female, she stood out. The street children were drawn to her because she returned, day after day.

She didn't ask anything of them or tell them to bathe. She simply wanted to show them love. Living as a missionary, she herself had very little to offer these orphans. In a way, this made it much easier for her to not focus so much on the physical need but the spiritual need.

The street orphans lacked trust, and given that the Philippines is steeped in idolatry, these children had no concept of God as their Father. Most of them didn't have good earthly fathers to serve as models. As Natalie did life with these children and taught them about the Bible, the children saw Jesus's love lived out. If Natalie had millions of dollars and gave these orphans anything their hearts desired, their physical needs would have been met beyond their wildest dreams. But by sharing the gospel with these street orphans, Natalie was giving them a gift that was far more important. She was giving them a gift that provides for all eternity regardless of what this life looks like. She offered them hope amidst despair.

Natalie, Brin, and eventually Natalie's husband, weren't embraced by everyone in that city. People knew who they were and what they were about. Pimps, drug dealers, and other unsavory characters lurked behind the scenes to watch what was going on. But God needed them there for a season to plant seeds in the dirt. Somebody needed to tell them that the lost are found and their debt has been paid. It wasn't always easy work (still isn't), but it was the work God called them to do. Because of their obedience, many came to know Christ as their Savior, and God as their Father. These once invisible orphans were adopted into God's family through their faith.

Seeds can spread and reproduce, but someone must first be willing to do the planting. The harvest is often the most plentiful where there are people who have nothing or very little. There must be someone willing to cultivate the soil. Jesus came for both the least and the greatest. If He could spend time with anybody and everybody, so must we.

Advocating for the Spiritual Orphan

1. Have you ever wanted to belong but didn't know where you belonged or with whom you belonged? Describe that experience.

2. Are you one who alienates people from your group, or do you seek to welcome new people into your community? Why or why not?

3. How do you think you would have responded to the woman we know as Photina before she encountered Christ? Would you have scorned her to her face, or would you have remained silent while others did? Is there someone in your life who is experiencing this kind of shunning? What are you doing about it?

4. Do you struggle with the idea that God loves you even when others don't? Is He enough for you?

5. Do you lash out at people because of loneliness or guilt? Or do you seek to share the gospel with everyone regardless of your circumstances or what people think of you?

Chapter Four

REMEMBER THE MISSION

THERE ARE PLENTY of spiritual leaders out there today who lead but don't always lead well. The difference between a leader who is leading well and one who is not is whether they are leading for man or for God. Are they leading to serve self or are they leading to serve God—to be obedient, humble, and most importantly, serve like Jesus served? This applies to every single person because we are all leading someone. Are we secure in who God says we are and in what we are called to do? Or are we insecure children looking for affirmation from whoever will throw it our way? Are we nurturing the next generation to spiritual success, or are we leaving a tidal wave of destruction in our wake?

I realize we are four chapters in, and we have covered some ground, but do you remember your commission? Being a Christian comes with some weighty responsibility.

> Therefore, if anyone is in Christ, the new creation
> has come: The old has gone, the new is here! All this
> is from God, who reconciled us to himself through
> Christ and gave us the ministry of reconciliation:
> that God was reconciling the world to himself in

Christ, not counting people's sins against them. And he has committed to us the message of recon- ciliation. We are therefore Christ's ambassadors, as though God were making his appeal through us.

—2 CORINTHIANS 5:17–20

You and I are Christ's ambassadors to sinners. We are the ones God has asked to spread this message of recon- ciliation. What are we to say to the spiritual orphan? *Be reconciled to God.*

———

In one of the greatest rescue missions in the Bible, we wit- ness the handiwork of a new leader trained under Moses. The scene looks like something out of a James Bond movie. Joshua secretly sent out two spies to scout the land God had promised them. Joshua ordered them to scout out the land on the other side of the Jordan River, especially around Jericho (Joshua 2:1). Upon their arrival in Jericho, the scouts got a room at the inn on the wall. Rahab was the innkeeper. Somehow, word got to the king that a couple of Israelites were in town to spy on them. Understandably, the people of Jericho were nervous because word had spread quickly about the Israelite's triumphs at the hands of their God (Joshua 2:9–10).

The king of Jericho immediately sent orders to Rahab to bring out the men. However, Rahab didn't quite tell the truth. She said she had seen them earlier, but they had left at dusk right before the city gates closed (Joshua 2:4–5). Rahab, not sure the king's men would believe her or not, hid the spies up on the roof under bundles of flax. The king's men bought her story and went searching for the spies along the road to the Jordan River.

Once Rahab felt confident the king's men were out of sight, she went upstairs and spoke with the spies. She said to them, "I know that the Lord has given you this land" (Joshua 2:9). Rahab knew without a doubt that the God of these spies was the supreme God of the heavens (Joshua 2:11). Rahab knew that in order for the Israelites to be given the land she occupied, it would have to be conquered. Conquering in that day meant destruction. She wanted to be assured by the spies that, because she acted in kindness to them by hiding them from the king's men, she and her family would be saved.

Not only did the spies say yes to Rahab's request, they offered their lives as a guarantee. These chosen, Israelite spies were having a discussion with a pagan woman who ran a brothel. And not only were they conversing with her, they said they would be willing to lose their lives should they not live up to their word. They didn't know when they checked into her little inn that they would have this conversation. It's a beautiful conversation because over the centuries since Christ hung on the cross, many people have had a similar unexpected conversation about a Man giving up His life for theirs as a fulfillment of His promise. And some of these conversations have taken place in a brothel too.

Rahab helped the spies escape, but before they left, the spies left her with some instructions. Rahab was required to leave hanging in her window the scarlet rope with which she let the spies down, and all of her relatives had to stay inside the house. If anyone went out in the street, they were on their own and would not be afforded any protection at that point (Joshua 2:19). The spies put their lives on the line should anyone in her home be touched. On the flip side, if Rahab betrayed the spies, the spies would no longer be bound by their oath.

After hiding out for three days as Rahab had instructed, the spies returned to Joshua and told him that the people in the land were scared of the Israelites. Several days and a few miracles later, the Israelites invaded Jericho. Joshua instructed the spies to keep their promise to Rahab and retrieve her and her family. The spies got them out safely and moved them to a safe place near Israel's camp (Joshua 6:23).

There's a shift that takes place between verses twenty-three and twenty-five. Verse twenty-three says that Rahab and her family live *near* the Israelites and verse twenty-five says Rahab lives *among* the Israelites. It's amazing grace. Not only did God save Rahab and her family, but He allowed them to live among His chosen people, and ultimately, Rahab played a huge role in the lineage of Jesus Christ. This mission over a thousand years before the promised Messiah displayed the splendor of the hope that would one day be available to all through the gospel.

Some scholars believe that one of the spies was Salmon, whom Rahab eventually married.[19] Salmon and Rahab had a son named Boaz (Ruth 4:21) who ended up marrying Ruth. Rahab was King David's great-great-grand-mother. All of this began because two spies rented a room at the inn of a prostitute, and they were kind and decent to one another. Each helped one another, and each kept their word. How very rare is that in today's society especially when people aren't of the same race, status, socioeconomic background, or lifestyle choice?

Every single one of God's created people is a rescue mission for Him. We are born separated from Him, and He will stop at nothing to save us and set us among His people. He keeps His word always. Sometimes when we struggle with people failing us, or failing to keep their word, we put God in the same box as them and think He might not come through either. It's sad, but true. Far too many people, even if they don't realize it, struggle with accepting that there is a God. And they don't realize their need for a Savior because they have been hurt so much by other people, and in many cases, their own fathers who failed to protect and provide.

I know what it's like to grow up fatherless. I never really knew my birth father. After my parents divorced when I was two years old, I saw my father only once when I was twenty years old for a total of seven days. There's a real struggle when you know only half of your story. When a piece is missing, it's noticeably missing. We are born with a desire for someone to care for us, and for us to belong to someone. I hated not knowing my father, and most of what I knew of him was through secondhand knowledge and based on my mom's experiences with him. Needless to say, those experiences weren't very good, or they wouldn't have divorced. I grew up missing a piece of what made me who I was. The stories I heard were told by someone else (if they were told at all), and I never had the opportunity to experience him for myself.

How many people also have this problem with God? God wired us with the need to desire Him, yet many don't know Him enough to know that He's the One they are searching for. Even worse, for some, what they do know about God is not good. They have someone else's stories to rely on without any firsthand experience with God. Even if you or I don't acknowledge or know either one of them, we all have a heavenly Father and an earthly father. For those whose experiences are not so great with their earthly father, they have a hard time understanding their heavenly Father is perfect. On the flip side, those who have a wonderful earthly father are sometimes tripped up when they begin to put their earthly fathers ahead of their heavenly Father.

Prior to accepting Christ as our Savior, we are all spiritual orphans because we are separated from our heavenly Father. Our sin separates us from His holiness. The Hebrew word for "orphan," *yathowm*, means "fatherless."[20] Children who were without a father were most at risk because women had no social or economic standing and struggled to provide for themselves unless they found someone else to marry them or care for them.

The same is true for all of us. We are at risk when we are Fatherless. Jesus said that no one gets to the Father except through Him (John 14:6). Those who are in Christ are charged with the task of taking Christ to the world so they can hear about Jesus, the Son of God, and the love of God, the Father.

Regardless of what some might claim or think, while every single person alive is part of God's creation, a person can only be an adopted child of God (Rom. 8:15) by accepting the free gift of salvation God offers through the death, burial, and resurrection of His Son, Jesus Christ. Before we acknowledge Jesus as Lord and Savior, we are all spiritual orphans doing life on our own terms. We can't ever forget this because if we forget the grace our sinful selves received, we will fail to extend that grace to others who desperately need it.

For so many years, I mourned the loss of my earthly father and all the possibilities. I tried to fill the gaping hole in my heart with worldly things and, at times, very sinful things. However, nothing filled the hole. I was an orphan looking for an earthly father who would provide, protect, and love me when I should have been looking to my heavenly Father because He fills all those roles perfectly. Regardless of my circumstances, His steadfastness and faithfulness remained constant even when things in my life did not. He was always pursuing me.

> He will sustain you to the end, so that you will be blameless on the day of our Lord Jesus Christ. God is faithful, who has called you into fellowship with his Son, Jesus Christ our Lord.
>
> —1 CORINTHIANS 1:8–9

Many have a hard time understanding that actions are associated with the condition of our heart. We have, ourselves, become a hardened, orphan generation. Our generation is known as "the fatherless generation" because of the fact so many children are being raised without fathers in the home who are actively engaged with their upbringing. Being fatherless creates a whole host of issues—behavioral, emotional, physical, and spiritual. Statistics show that children who are raised without fathers have an increased risk of joblessness, homelessness, suicide, addiction, and participating in crime.[21]

Instead of seeing the root of the problem with a child (the fact the father is absent), we tend to focus on the physical response to this pain. We focus on the child, who eventually grows up to be an adult, all wrong. We look at their actions instead of their hearts. Have we taken the time to ask them about their hearts? Have we told them how much Jesus loves them?

I am always in awe of those who are called to prison ministry. I've often begged God not to send me into this mission field. It causes me to think anxious thoughts about voluntarily entering a physical environment with so many people convicted of incredibly horrible things. My mind immediately moves to a scenario where a prison riot occurs when I am in the facility. It's completely irrational, I know, but it makes me hyperventilate even as I type these words.

Dear friends of mine spend time every single month going into prisons and leading Bible studies, worship services, and prayer events. Some of the prisoners have accepted Jesus, but many show up out of curiosity. For some, it's simply a momentary respite from the hard days of prison. The Bible says, "For where two or three gather in my name, there am I with them" (Matt. 18:20). The presence of the Holy Spirit fills prisons as believers gather. Jesus doesn't stay on the outside of the prison afraid to rub shoulders with the prisoners. He doesn't care about a potential lockdown, Jesus is never one to shy away from being with the people who need Him the most.

Not only is Jesus there when my friends are serving the prisoners, but He remains long after they leave. How? Because men and women—seen as convicted criminals to most of the world—are seen and loved by Jesus. They've given their lives to Jesus and because they have, Jesus declares them part of the royal priesthood—brothers and sisters to the saints all around the world—even as they live out their days within prison walls.

That's not an easy pill for us to swallow, right? Criminals, including prostitutes like Rahab, have the same standing with Jesus as those who have never stepped foot into a prison cell? Yes, they do. And if God loves them as His own, we must love them as our brothers and sisters as well.

> But you are a chosen people, a royal priesthood, a holy nation, God's special possession, that you may declare the praises of him who called you out of darkness into his wonderful light.
>
> —1 PETER 2:9

My friends go into the prisons not to pour on shame and judgment but to tell the condemned that Jesus has paid the ultimate price for their sins. They go into a dark place filled with violence and despair shining their lights brightly for all to see. They offer hugs to those who may have never felt the hug of a father. To them, it's a rescue mission.

The person's crime may cause them to be known in this world as a convicted felon, but Jesus says He can use them regardless of what the world says about them. Jesus pursues men and women in prison cells the same as He does men and women in boardrooms, courtrooms, businesses, or homes. He loves everyone the same, and so should we.

I was recently watching an old episode of *M.A.S.H.*[22] In it, Colonel Potter had a hard conversation with an old friend. The officer Colonel Potter was talking to had left his office job in Washington, DC, so he could earn his combat medal. Problem is, the guy wasn't combat ready. He had sat behind a desk for years. Instead of acknowledging his lack of experience and recognizing his problem as pride, he led a battalion of young soldiers into battle and the team suffered many casualties and injuries. Even after being injured, this prideful officer wanted to return to battle because he had only four more days to earn his combat medal for his retirement benefits. Colonel Potter said, "No way." Why? Because Colonel Potter was concerned that even if only one young soldier died under the officer's care over that four-day period, it was one too many.

To lose one is too many. Do you feel this way? If even one person dies today not knowing the Lord regardless of their background, does this burden you? If even one person falls into the abyss of darkness here on Earth, does it warrant your time? God says it should because He never wants to lose even one. Would you put your own life on the line for "the one" like the spies did for Rahab and her family?

> Then Jesus told them this parable: "Suppose one of you has a hundred sheep and loses one of them. Doesn't he leave the ninety-nine in the open country and go after the lost sheep until he finds it? And when he finds it, he joyfully puts it on his shoulders and goes home. Then he calls his friends and neighbors together and says, 'Rejoice with me; I have found my lost sheep.' I tell you that in the same way there will be more rejoicing in heaven over one sinner who repents than over ninety-nine righteous persons who do not need to repent."
>
> —LUKE 15:3–7

We make it so easy for people to check out and continue to live in sin, making bad choices. We are afraid to share the gospel and God's Word with people. We say, "It's up to you whether you belong to a church community."

But it's not OK. If we don't share these things with people, who will? We expect someone else to do the job and, sadly, that someone else is often Satan who distorts what God says. God doesn't tell Christians to back down. His Spirit gives us power to be bold and courageous like Peter after the day of Pentecost.[23] If He didn't want us to do this, we'd have no need for the Holy Spirit to reside within us and Jesus would have never issued the Great

Commission.[24] It's OK to be this in-your-face (I like to call it compassionate) with your people. How do I know this? Because one day we will be held accountable to God.

What if one day God asks, "Why did you never tell the orphan that they have a Father?" I don't know about you, but I don't want God asking me that question. Do you?

Christians bear the duty of living a life that reflects Christ in everything we do. This includes daily picking up our cross and leading others to the gospel. It's not an option for the believer. Salvation is about getting into heaven. However, sanctification is about being grateful for the gift of salvation and using that gratefulness and humility to lead others to Christ just as you yourself were led.

If I'm doing what God has called me to do, you are doing what God has called you to do, and someone else is doing what God has called them to do, the kingdom has more coverage. Sit out or forfeit, and we'll lose every time. It feels a little as though our generation is losing all too often these days because too many are sitting out when God has asked them to reach out instead.

God pursued me for a very long time. I heard Him and often ignored Him. Admittedly, there were times I even mocked Him. I was a sinner in need of a Savior. During a woman-at-the-well kind of moment, God sent a spiritual father to me to deliver His message of grace. This encounter changed my life. It has also been a huge blessing to have this relationship even today as I do life. He's the person I call when I need to talk and dream, and when I need godly counsel.

I sometimes wonder what would have happened to me had this spiritual father not walked into my life at just the right time and rescued me. What if he had chosen disobedience and stayed home? What if he had taken the easy road and not started a conversation with me that night? What if he didn't speak up when God gave him a word of knowledge?

I'm so thankful for his complete obedience to the Holy Spirit because it changed everything about my life. Not only did he invest in me that night, he, along with his wife, have been my spiritual parents for almost eleven years. I don't see them often, but we talk often, and I know they pray for me and my family. A conversation with them never lasts less than two hours, and we never talk about the weather. It is always Spirit-filled conversation and always includes instruction, prophesy, encouragement, and prayer.

Let me assure you, this is not some elderly couple with lots of time on their hands. They are the parents of five grown children and a bazillion grandchildren, great-grandchildren, and one great-great-grandchild. They are still active in ministry and have lots of spiritual children around the world. They love and lead well because they love Jesus above all else.

I'm still not entirely sure how it happened, but last spring, we became the proud owners of some chickens. We don't live in a rural area. We live in the city, but apparently, our large city is rather chicken-friendly. Who knew?

I'll be honest; I have no idea how to raise chickens or take care of chickens, so I leave that up to my google-savvy teenage son who wanted the chickens in the first place. We started out with five hens. I knew enough not to start out with chicks; that's a lot more work. The original five settled in relatively quickly. The older hens picked on one of the younger chickens in the beginning, but nothing too major.

Eleven short days later, we were giddy with joy when one of the hens laid her first egg. We weren't the only ones. We noticed that over time, the hens would appear to cheer one another on when one went near the nesting box or when one by one, they all started laying eggs. It was as if they had a congratulatory party every single day. I thought it was cute and endearing. I had no idea what any of their noise actually meant.

We had peace in the coop until we introduced hens number six and seven. I'm not sure how things like this transpire around my home. I mean, isn't five chickens enough? We were told to separate the two new hens until dusk and then put them in the coop. We were told that it is challenging to integrate chickens into a new environment with other chickens during the daylight hours. It's best for the chickens to be surprised and wake up with the new hens in the coop. So. Many. Moving. Parts.

While we had hens six and seven separated in a small cage awaiting dusk, the older (and much bigger) hen pecked the younger chicken so hard that she drew blood and took out feathers. I was heartbroken. Our other five happy chickens had pecked at one another but had never drawn blood. I thought, "What did we get ourselves into? Maybe it was just the small space and the stress of the move."

That was wishful thinking. What we ended up doing was somehow getting two new chickens that were now the oldest and the youngest, respectively, in the coop. The oldest hen has a beak that is super big and very sharp. She drew blood on another hen on day two and another one on day three. The third incident occurred while in the nesting box. There was so much blood in the nesting box that it looked like a crime scene.

I snapped a picture and sent it to my son who in turn asked the chicken whisperer guy if everything was OK. He said, "Looks fine to me. It's hard to watch for some people, but if they weren't acting this way, it wouldn't be normal."

I'm that some people!

I've shed tears over these chickens trying to figure out their positioning in the coop. At times, I've yelled their names to avoid an attack (seriously, can a chicken even learn its name?). I've pleaded with my son to separate them because I feel so bad, especially for the youngest one who frantically sprints through the coop lest anyone peck and chase her.

Through all of this, what I've discovered is that the "pecking order" is a real thing. Chickens establish a pecking order within their space, and they will do anything to keep their position.

My tender heart has a hard time with it all.

It reminds me of children on a school playground trying to assert dominance or insecure people in a work environment. And, even though it shouldn't, it also makes me think of people in the church.

When we run around pecking at people trying to assert our dominance or rightful place in the kingdom, we run the risk of hurting people—sending some into the corner to hide and hurting some so bad they must leave and find safe shelter somewhere else. Just as I worry whether my baby hen Olive is getting any food or water, I wonder if those who can't find their place in the church risk dying of hunger and thirst because they aren't invited in or don't feel welcome in the place they should belong more than anywhere else.

I wish Christians were more like pack animals and not so much like pecking-order animals. Packs need and rely on each other; pecking orders, not so much. If Christians are to look different and not look like the world, we can't be the people who tear others down to elevate ourselves. We shouldn't try and look better than other brothers and sisters. We should come alongside those brothers and sisters and see how we can help them in their battles. Most importantly, Christians can't peck at those who are seeking.

If the Holy Spirit is drawing a person to the Father, we must let them not only get to the door but also allow them inside. Sideways glances and whispers amongst ourselves will never make a person feel welcomed. Asking them to change their outward appearance before they experience an inward change will never work, and even then, we need to be careful.

Jesus loved people right where they were in life.

- The grungy fishermen—they followed him stinky and all.

- The woman with the issue of blood—Jesus wasn't concerned at all that she had touched him.

- The lepers' sores weren't an issue for Jesus.

- The prostitute who washed Jesus's feet let her hair down—Jesus didn't even mention it.

None of these outward things bothered Jesus. His only concern was their hearts.

Jesus said, "You like to appear righteous in public, but God knows your hearts. What this world honors is detestable in the sight of God" (Luke 16:15, NLT).

My chickens don't care if they hurt the other chickens' hearts because all they are concerned with is being at the top of the pecking order. We, Christians, are not to act like chickens. We are to be like Jesus. Jesus voluntarily chose to leave the right hand of God the Father to come to Earth and love the least. We need to love the least like Jesus does, and we need to agree that there is no place for a pecking order in the kingdom of God.

Jesus quickly shut down a pecking order notion when James and John asked to be seated at the right and left side of Jesus. It's a good thing for James and John that the ten disciples who heard their request had been changed by spending time with Jesus! Jesus's response to their request was priceless: "You want to be the greatest? Then you must become the servant. Are you willing to do that?" (Mark 10:35–45, author's paraphrase).

May we spend more energy and time remembering the mission. May we welcome people in instead of trying to box them out or make them feel less than worthy to get to Jesus. There is only One who sits at the top of the pack in the kingdom of God. The rest of us are merely brothers and sisters who need one another in this life. As the writer of Hebrews said, "Let us think of ways to motivate one another to acts of love and good works. And let us not neglect our meeting together, as some people do, but encourage one another, especially now that the day of his return is drawing near" (Heb. 10:24–25, NLT).

And, not only do we need one another, we've been commanded not to stay in our safe, Christian coops but to reach out to those who need to hear about Jesus. It's a daunting task for a chicken to leave its coop, but once they become brave, they realize God gave them the ability to do something their predators can't do— fly. When in danger, the chicken will fly up onto a roost or into a tree.

Friend, God gave you the gift of the Holy Spirit to help you feel brave enough to witness to and

> *Grace doesn't sell; you can hardly give it away, because it works only for losers and no one wants to stand in their line. The world of winners...will not buy free forgiveness because that threatens to let the riffraff into the Supper of the Lamb.*[25]
>
> — ROBERT CAPON

love on the spiritual orphan. He will give you eyes to see the person as He sees the person. We shouldn't be afraid of those who aren't like us or believe something different than us. Instead, we need to learn to rely on the Holy Spirit to help us get outside of our comfort zones so that we can share about Jesus and cheer on many new believers in the faith.

Advocating for the Spiritual Orphan

1. When you think of "the one" Jesus came to save, who comes to mind?

2. Do you believe the worst sinners in the world have the same equal access to Jesus as you do? Do you believe some are just too far gone for Him to save?

3. Are you making yourself available to reach the downtrodden and outcasts of society? Or are you only engaged with comfortable ministry?

4. If you could do one thing this year that you deemed to be radical ministry work, what would it be? What is holding you back from doing it?

Chapter Five

CHANGE YOUR LANGUAGE

I SAT ACROSS FROM a woman one morning whom I just met the night before and she spoke words into my hurting soul. She said, "I am going to need you to change your language." She referred to something I had said earlier in our conversation. Simply by pointing out the words I used to describe someone important in my life, her critique changed my spiritual perspective on everything. Where once I felt like I was constantly bumping up against a stone wall, it was as if God had created a doorway in the stone right there in that coffee shop.

Satan distorts and trips us up all the time. He twists and manipulates Scripture like nobody else can. "Did God really say...?" is his go-to line. If we are not careful, Satan will distort our image of the very people God knit together in the womb. When we stop seeing people for their potential in Christ and instead look only at their future potential trip to hell, we need to repent and seek forgiveness. Hell and brimstone preaching doesn't work unless the gospel is presented as an option. Simply screaming

> *Perhaps God needs you to change your language as it relates to the spiritual orphan.*

at someone in their sin and telling them they are going to hell gets no one anywhere, including you. Instead of screaming at people or speaking ill of them behind their backs, we need to change our language.

Other than salvation, do you know what one of the great things about being a Christian is? Prayer. Prayer is the place where heaven and Earth unite. As believers, we are afforded the right to enter with boldness into the presence of God through prayer (Heb. 4:16). This access should not be taken lightly and should not be undertaken without understanding the risk. If prayer is the place where heaven and Earth unite, it is also the place where darkness and light do battle.

———————

After the May 2017 terror attack at an Ariana Grande concert in Manchester, England, many people felt angry, fearful, and confused. The attacker went after children when he blew himself up just outside the concert doors. Parents, waiting for their children, were maimed and killed. The youngest victim of the bombing was just eight years old.[26]

A few days after the attack, I was scanning through my Facebook timeline. A friend had posted an article about this incident. The author, a man, was angry and his anger was pointed at ISIS. However, his approach was completely off the mark. His battle cry, "The only appropriate reaction is righteous fury that turns to a grim determination to exact a retribution upon the bomber's bros so thorough and so comprehensive that in a thousand years the few descendants of the survivors will still terrify their children with the story of the vengeance exacted by the avengers of the West."[27]

Yikes! I sure hope this guy isn't a Christian because if he is, he has completely lost the compassion to share the gospel and to love one's enemies. We can't lead anyone to the Lord if we are enacting vengeance upon them.

My response to my friend about this man's post was this:

> We've only ever had one enemy. Sure, he manifests himself differently in different generations, but he still has power in this world. Sadly, many are fighting this fight in the physical where it can't be won. We don't have enough strength to win this way. This is a spiritual problem revealing itself in the physical. It's a lack of fearing God and removing Him as our only priority. These radicals have been around for thousands of years, and they were born out of disobedience and arrogance against God. We can use words on paper or around the water cooler to try and fight this battle, or we can drop to our knees in prayer, seek forgiveness, and be intentional about ministering to spiritual orphans (those who are separated from the Father) to lead them home.

We must redirect our energy because "We are not fighting against flesh-and-blood enemies, but against evil rulers and authorities of the unseen world, against mighty powers in this dark world, and against evil spirits in the heavenly places" (Eph. 6:12, NLT).

Mocking prayer has become common fodder among politicians, media, late-night comedians, and celebrities. Instead of relying on God, people lean heavily on what man can do (regulations, training, and the like). People are missing the mark and don't quite realize that with man, nothing is possible, but with God, all things are possible (Matt. 19:26). Below are some of the statements that have circulated after significant events such as school shootings and terrorist attacks occur.

"Prayer isn't working."

"Thoughts and prayers are nice, but they aren't going to change things."

"God isn't fixing this!"

The author of the three statements above is not God; the author is Satan. Every single one of these statements is the opposite of what God says in His Word. Because

- He waits for our prayers (Phil. 4:6–7; 1 Pet. 3:12; 1 John 5:15).

- Our prayers change things (James 5:14–16; Eph. 6:18).

- God is in complete control (Luke 12:22–27; Rev. 1:17).

Throughout the plagues God inflicted upon Pharaoh and the people of Egypt during the time of Moses, a phrase stands out. It was repeated over and over during all but the plague of darkness and the death of Egypt's firstborn. (See Exodus 7–10.) Pharaoh would not release the Israelites, a plague would come (horrible plagues that increased in severity), Pharaoh would ask Moses to stop the plague, Moses would plead to the Lord on Egypt's behalf, and the plague would end.

Reread that. Moses would plead to the Lord on their behalf. He prayed for the ones inflicting the torment upon the Israelites by continuing to enslave them and deny them the opportunity to go into the wilderness to worship.

God required Moses to pray for the Egyptians. God was in complete control, but He wouldn't act until Moses did his part. God required both physical action and prayer. Moses had to go to Pharaoh and make the demands. God hardened Pharaoh's heart. God knew exactly how the story was going to play out.

The truth for us today is that God knows how the story in our generation is going to play out. He knows what is to come, and He is in total control. The question for us today is, "Are we participating in His plan through prayer?" Even when prayer doesn't appear to be making a difference, I would hate to think what our world might look like today without the prayers of those who came before us (prayers prayed many years ago) and the prayers of today's people.

Don't stop praying. Don't let Satan win. Commit to being even more intentional with your prayers. Be specific. Pray for people by name. Pray for cities, schools, neighborhoods, and the hard issues we are facing. Ask in His name for good things to happen—miraculous, supernatural things. Don't ask for these things as a sign to prove His faithfulness. But instead ask for these things as an offering of your faith. God is waiting, and He is always listening.

> I call on you, my God, for you will answer me; turn your ear to me and hear my prayer.
>
> —PSALM 17:6

I do not type the words in this book with a lighthearted attitude. I type these words with fear and trembling because I know the cost of the battle I have signed up for. I am claiming what author Jennifer Eivaz says about spiritual battles with higher-ranking spirits: "When God gives you an assignment, He gives you authority for the assignment."[28] The authority shouldn't be handled presumptuously but should be in partnership with the Holy Spirit.

I'm convinced the crisis we are facing in this generation is spiritual because nothing is new under the sun (Eccl. 1:9). As I read through the Old Testament, time and time again every battle fought in the physical was either won or lost in the spiritual. The results of every single physical act of war or hardship was a consequence of the spiritual things (the things God told them to do) the people did or did not do. Every. Single. One. Every leader who did what was right in the sight of the Lord always had favor, and every leader who did not do what was right in the sight of the Lord was always the source of leading the people astray and straight into destruction.

Media.

It's the hot topic of right now. So much media and so much noise. As I read Joel chapters one and two recently, the word *solemn* jumped out at me. In these chapters, the Lord gave a call to repentance. He saw the vile behavior and the hardened, rebellious hearts, yet He was still willing to give the people another chance. God said to blow the trumpet, call a fast, call a solemn assembly, assemble the elders, gather the children, and cry out for mercy (Joel 2:15–17).

Solemn generally means to have a seriousness to something. When I think of solemn, I think of the opposite of spectacle and show. It makes me think about our national days of prayer and our acts of worship. Somehow these things have become a show in and of themselves. These events are perfectly planned, perfectly scripted, and perfectly timed with so many cameras and so much movement. I've yet to see anyone fully lamenting and laying bare their soul and concern for the country. When I think of the type of assembly the Lord was calling the people to in the Book of Joel, I don't picture what we see today.

I recently posted the following on social media:

> Every time the words *sound the trumpets* appear in the Bible, it is a call to the people of God to gather for and engage in battle. It's about time that we, Christians, stop battling against one another and remember who we represent...Jesus.
>
> Let's engage in the spiritual battle that is taking place all around us by praying, pressing into His Word, and living out His commands to love Him and love others. Let's give up our comforts and our

agendas and remember what His plan is: to praise Him all our days and to share the Gospel with people...every single person; not just some people or those we feel like sharing the Gospel with, but each person He came to die for. Remember, He loved you when you were a sinner far from Him.

The trumpets are sounding all around us. This generation is a mess and in a fight for its life. Are you willing to give in and fall prey to the things of this world or are you ready to join the battle to revive a generation like no other time before in history? The battle is not won with our words hurled at people, but it is won in our hearts. If you love people enough and care about this world, your nation, your city, your family, your friends, and your neighbor, the darkness in this world should alarm you. The great news is that it is never too dark for God's light to penetrate.

How about instead of yelling at people and cursing those who are in the darkness, we shine our lights really bright so the spiritual orphans can find their way home to their Father? He can change anyone's heart just like He did with yours.

We have a serious problem in this country (as is true for many countries around the world), and we are spiraling out of control. Natural disasters are ravishing our land, and our people are being devoured by one another. At some point, enough is enough. In the grand scheme of things, hateful and frustrated words toward one another don't matter, protesting doesn't matter, and even votes don't matter. What matters is that we gather together, weep, mourn, fast, and pray to the Lord to soften our hearts and the hearts of others. And most importantly, we need to hope the Lord sees our repentance as holy and acceptable before His eyes and delivers us from this path of self-induced destruction.

I'm tired of waking up to reports of mass shootings, stories of parents killing their children, accounts of innocent people killed while driving because someone was under the influence of something, news of chaos in the White House, unrelenting media, angry and violent protesters, escalating divorce rates, drunkenness abounding, the ease at which we legalize mind-altering drugs and alcohol, overpopulated prisons, and the list goes on and on. As I stare at this list, none of it is what God prescribes. There isn't an ounce of love in any of it.

Just typing the list brings a wave of sorrow.

What can you and I do? Let us solemnly assemble—anyone who is tired of the chaos—and watch what the Lord will do. No media, no hype. Let us blow the trumpet and gather for one purpose: to let the Lord know how sorry we are that we've messed up and allowed Him to be replaced. It is certainly not the first time in history this has happened.

> "Look closely. Has this ever happened before, That a nation has traded in its gods for gods that aren't even close to gods? But my people have traded my Glory for empty god-dreams and silly god-schemes. Stand in shock, heavens, at what you see! Throw up your hands in disbelief—this can't be!" GOD'S DECREE. "My people have committed a compound

sin: they've walked out on me, the fountain of fresh
flowing waters, and then dug cisterns—cisterns that
leak, cisterns that are no better than sieves."
—Jeremiah 2:11–13, the Message

Let us not be the generation in America that is marked
by rebellion and destruction or mocked by unbelievers.
Let us instead be the generation that is remembered for
its dependence upon the Lord like no other generation in
history. We are spiritually bankrupt, and our manmade
cisterns are disintegrating by the moment. The writer in
Hebrews challenges the people to warn each other every
day while it is still "today" (Heb. 3:13). Why? Because a
few lines before that, the writer reiterated the words God
spoke to Moses about the people never being able to enter
into His rest because of their hardened and rebellious
hearts (Heb. 3:10–11).

I don't know about you, but I am much more inclined
to want His eternal rest and peace than to live in a world
of chaos and destruction. I hope you are too. We need to
pray for more opportunities for the gospel to go forward—
not opportunities to share about agendas, beliefs, and poli-
cies—because the gospel is the only thing that changes
people from the inside out.

Let us pray that the people who know and love Jesus
will gather (shepherds, gather your sheep). Let us also pray
that the people who are far from Jesus will gather with us
because the Spirit can reach hearts when we gather and
invite Him into our presence.

A few years ago, I was standing at the counter shucking corn when a couple thoughts entered my mind, "Where are my children, and why are they not helping me?" I mean, shucking corn was the highlight of summer for me when I was a child. I loved shucking corn. A few minutes later, more thoughts crept in: "Am I preparing my children well for adulthood? Does a simple task like shucking corn matter in the grand scheme of things? Are they missing out?"

All of this over a few pieces of corn!

Do you have thoughts like these too? I so hope I am not alone! As my initial thoughts simmered down, I asked myself more questions: "What didn't I do as a child that my mom did? Is it affecting me as an adult? Will there even be corn to shuck when my children are preparing dinner one day for their families? Why is the world changing so fast? What are the most important things I need to teach my children?"

Shucking corn was a fond summer memory for me as was riding my bike around the neighborhood and coming in when the streetlights came on. My children don't do any of those things either. I loved reading books and watching Saturday morning cartoons (because Saturday was the only day cartoons were on). Now, there are thousands of channels and online streaming available, books on gadgets, and audiobooks. I plead with my children to put down their electronics in exchange for a paperback, and I find myself forcing them into the backyard to play.

Daily, I find myself getting caught up in the small things—like the fact my kids don't shuck corn with me or spend countless hours reading because there is nothing else to do. I don't think I am alone. I believe many of us try to compare yesteryear to today, and honestly, it just doesn't work. Things and times change. Well, at least some things.

For some time now, I've had something stirring inside of me. I have been patiently waiting to see how it was going to manifest and when it was appropriate to share. It gets me so fired up and excited that it is often too difficult to contain it. Within our church, community, nation, and even the world, we've been asking God to send revival. We've been pleading. We've been organizing prayer meetings and organizing "revival" events. We've been seeking.

And you know what? God hears our prayers! He is responding! God opened up the heavens over two thousand years ago. He is answering prayers at rapid speed. The blind see, the lost are found, and prisoners are set free. The Lord is waging war from the heavens against those who seek to harm His children.

Do we honestly believe this? Do we know it in our core? Sometimes I don't think we do. I am not artistic at all, but if I was, I would draw a cartoon to illustrate what I believe happens in heaven sometimes when it comes to revival here on Earth. Picture this, God, Jesus, and the Holy Spirit (the three-in-one blessed Trinity) conversing about our plea:

God: "Jesus, Son, I've heard the people's prayers and I have given them what they have been asking for, but they keep asking for the same thing. Why do you think that is?"

Jesus: "Father, I have no idea. Maybe you should ask the Holy Spirit. He lives in them."

Holy Spirit: "Jesus, you are always asking me this same question. I whisper the answers to them. I point them in the right direction. They just keep asking for You to come again quickly."

I've struggled with this myself. Do I want revival— including all the work and sacrifice that comes along with it—or do I just want Jesus to return so we can be done with this whole messy world?

In seeking answers, I've gone through Scripture and history books about past revival events. I've read about the First and Second Great Awakenings, the Azusa Street Revival, D. L. Moody's amazing ministry, and the works of Charles G. Finney, among others. You know what I found? Although they look similar but different, do you know the one similarity they all share is that they started with a person. A person burdened enough to seek the Lord through prayer.

Every day, I am amazed at

> *Revival begins when you draw a circle around yourself and make sure everything in that circle is right with God.*[29]
> —ANNE GRAHAM LOTZ

the work the Lord is doing in this world. I can pull up my Facebook feed and my Twitter account and see the many ministries in my city and around the world that are making a difference and leading people to Jesus Christ. It is not one person every month or so giving their lives to Christ. There is life change happening every single day in large numbers. What would D. L. Moody have done with hundreds of thousands of followers on Twitter? What would people have said about a revival event during the Second Great Awakening that had thirty thousand in attendance? These are the numbers we have every day around the world. Yet, we think revival isn't happening? Seriously!

We can't just pray for revival; we need to actively seek to see His kingdom come. We need to be engaged in the work God is doing. It needs to get us excited and cause us to lose sleep. We need to be focused on prayer and loving people. Very rarely did God do all the work in the battles we read about in the Bible. Prayer—a conversation with God—was always the first step. The second step required action, sometimes unusual action, to complete God's mission.

Iranians are being baptized in their country despite the threat of persecution. I have friends serving the people of Uganda who are responding to the gospel because someone was willing to be there and share it with them. I've attended youth events where hundreds of teens surrendered to Jesus. ISIS in Mosul pushed Christians out, but I think God moved them out for a far greater purpose than we can even imagine or ask for. And there is so much more! God is moving globally!

We must be willing to open our eyes to see what God is doing. Psalm 69:32 says, "When the humble see it they will be glad; you who seek God, let your hearts revive." As we seek Him, God opens our eyes to the fact He has already opened the heavens. We can't see heaven through the natural eye. We can only see heaven through the supernatural eye. My spiritual momma once said to me, "God has opened up the heavens. Ask for *big* things. Be bold."

> The LORD will open to you his good treasury, the heavens, to give the rain to your land in its season and to bless all the work of your hands. And you shall lend to many nations, but you shall not borrow.
> —DEUTERONOMY 28:12

Our goal on Earth should not be to please ourselves but to bring glory to God. If you are willing, God will use you as a vessel to bring His glorious message of salvation to the spiritual orphan. Anyone who is not in a saving, personal relationship with Jesus is separated from their heavenly Father. This includes your child, parent, sweet little grandma and grandpa, friend, the grocery store clerk, government representatives, enemies, and those who abide in some other religion or belief outside of Jesus Christ.

This issue of being spiritually separated is not new. The prophet Ezekiel had an encounter with God about the state of the nation of Israel in his time (Ezek. 37:1–14).

The hand of the Lord was upon me, and he brought me out in the Spirit of the Lord and set me down in the middle of the valley; it was full of bones. And he led me around among them, and behold, there were very many on the surface of the valley, and behold, they were very dry. And he said to me, "Son of man, can these bones live?" And I answered, "O Lord God, you know." Then he said to me, "Prophesy over these bones, and say to them, O dry bones, hear the word of the Lord. Thus says the Lord God to these bones: Behold, I will cause breath to enter you, and you shall live. And I will lay sinews upon you, and will cause flesh to come upon you, and cover you with skin, and put breath in you, and you shall live, and you shall know that I am the Lord."

So I prophesied as I was commanded. And as I prophesied, there was a sound, and behold, a rattling, and the bones came together, bone to its bone. And I looked, and behold, there were sinews on them, and flesh had come upon them, and skin had covered them. But there was no breath in them. Then he said to me, "Prophesy to the breath; prophesy, son of man, and say to the breath, Thus says the Lord God: Come from the four winds, O breath, and breathe on these slain, that they may live." So I prophesied as he commanded me, and the breath came into them, and they lived and stood on their feet, an exceedingly great army.

Then he said to me, "Son of man, these bones are the whole house of Israel. Behold, they say, 'Our bones are dried up, and our hope is lost; we are indeed cut off.' Therefore prophesy, and say to them, Thus says the Lord God: Behold, I will open your graves and raise you from your graves, O my people. And I will bring you into the land of Israel. And you shall know that am the Lord, when I open your graves, and raise you from your graves, O my people. And I will put my Spirit within you, and you shall live, and I will place you in your own land. Then you shall know that I am the Lord; I have spoken, and I will do it, declares the Lord."

—ESV

God has revealed our "dry bones." The Word went out and continues to go out and people will be saved before the return of the Lord. We need to stop praying for revival because it is already here right in front of our faces every single day! If He answered our prayers for a new car by giving us one, you better bet we'd be out driving that new baby around! If we are not careful, the embers of the revival flame will burn out and we will miss the opportunity to be a part of *History.* Please don't miss out! Engage. Be a part of something bigger than yourself.

Friend, may your dry bones have life breathed into them and may revival engage your heart into action for the spiritual orphan. We are living under an open heaven. Praise God!

A few years have passed since I stood shucking corn at my kitchen counter asking myself the questions I mentioned earlier. What started as a simple domestic chore launched me into a mini-revival right there in my kitchen. However, so much has happened in this world since that night. It seems chaos is abounding more, and Christians are grasping at straws instead of tethering themselves to hope. We can't afford to go down with the ship because people's lives are at stake.

Grab a hold of your life-preserver (Jesus), and He will get you back into the boat and set your feet on solid ground. Maybe, like Peter, God wants to do a recommissioning work in you right now. Let Him revive your heart and speak words of affirmation over you so you can get back into action.

Advocating for the Spiritual Orphan

1. Are you actively praying for the ones the world says are evil, wicked, and our enemies? If you are not, why?

2. How can you be more like Moses in your prayer life? Do you want to intercede more for others, or do you think it is too much work and not worth your time?

3. Do you care about the well-being of others? Do you care that some will die today without knowing Jesus as their Lord and Savior? Why or why not?

4. Are you waiting for a "revival" moment, or are you living revival every day?

Chapter Six

WINDOWS TO OUR SOULS

EMEMBER WHEN I told you about the man God sent into my life to speak a word of knowledge to me? The word he spoke through the nudging of the Holy Spirit profoundly impacted me that day. However, what I first noticed about him was not what he said, it was the way his eyes looked. His eyes were like deep blue pools of fresh water. I was in a thirsty season hungering for truth, and what this man possessed behind those eyes is what I longed for.

The Bible tells us many things about our eyes, and the thing I love (or hate depending on what season of my life I am in) is what our eyes reflect about the health of our soul. When I first met this man, his eyes drew me in. What he saw in my eyes confirmed for him that this was not a chance meeting but instead was a God-arranged encounter. He saw my troubled soul reflected in my eyes that day. He saw the darkness I felt.

I didn't know anything about what he saw in my eyes that day until the next morning. After my radical encounter with Jesus and the Holy Spirit the previous night, I was changed. I knew it. I believed it. My new friend saw it. When I saw him at breakfast that morning, he looked in my eyes and said, "The darkness has been removed. Now all I see is light." Mind you, I was a newborn believer and had never had anyone deliver a word of knowledge to me, pray for me, or lead me in the sinner's prayer. I didn't know what it meant to have an encounter with the Holy Spirit, and I never had someone speak of the condition of my soul before. It was a little uncomfortable, but it was God's way of getting my attention.

I didn't know this man very long before I figured out who he was. His name is Albie Pearson.[30] He played for Major League baseball in the late 1950s and early 1960s. He was known throughout the league for his short stature. He played hard and lived hard. An encounter with Jesus changed his life, but he ran in the shadows of the dugout and no one dared speak about their faith lest they be thought of as odd, weird, or a troublemaker.

The death of an American icon fueled Albie's passion for ministry, especially toward youth. In the spring of 1962, Albie had the opportunity to escort Marilyn Monroe onto the field before a game to receive a charity donation. Albie said Marilyn was the loneliest person he ever saw in his life. She turned on her charm and her character in the spotlight, but as quickly as the lights faded as she made her way back to the dugout, her smile immediately vanished. Albie found himself staring into Marilyn's searching eyes. Instead of turning from him, her eyes stared right back at him as she said, "What is it that you are trying to tell me?" Albie opened his mouth but said nothing.

After this night, Marilyn Monroe never made another public appearance. Several weeks later, Albie heard that

Marilyn Monroe died of a drug overdose. The news crippled Albie and later that night, he fell to his knees in his hotel room. He knew he wasn't the cause of her death, but he had been given an opportunity to share the hope of Jesus with Marilyn and he didn't take it. As he cried out to God, he made a promise that he wouldn't allow that to happen ever again and he asked God to give him the courage and the strength to share his faith for the rest of his life.[31]

God answered that prayer, and Albie stayed true to his promise. How do I know? Because the minute I met him, Albie, with his welcoming eyes and soft tone, walked right up to me and said, "Jesus loves you, Erin."

Many people before me heard these same words spoken by Albie and his wife, Helen.

After a career-ending injury forced his retirement in 1966, Albie and Helen birthed a youth ministry out of their modest home in Riverside, CA. They welcomed all. Even the drug dealers knew him as "preacher man" and dumped "deadbeats" on their porch. Albie and Helen cared for the youth as their own. They lived out spiritual parenthood for the struggling youth in their area.

Albie went on to plant churches through his international ministry. In 1997, he and Helen founded Father's Heart Ranch, a group home for abused and neglected boys.[32] Albie knew that the only way to reach the youth was to help them understand how much their heavenly Father loves them. They accomplished this task by living out love toward these boys and sharing the Word of God with them.

You and I may never have the opportunity to share the gospel with a celebrity, plant churches, or open a group home, but you and I have opportunities. Every day, we bump shoulders with people who are hurting, lonely, desperate, and separated from God. Are we taking the time to look people in their eyes to see the condition of their soul? Or are we walking around with blinders on our own eyes because spiritual work is hard, difficult, and sometimes downright uncomfortable?

Instead of always loving as Christ did, we want to protect ourselves from the dirtiness of this world, and by doing so, we withhold extending His story of grace and salvation from those whom we choose not to invest our time into or love. May we respond to the Holy Spirit's nudges to motivate us to actually do something.

God dropped a nugget of affirmation on me one morning during my neighborhood Bible study. The ladies and I were discussing deep wells versus shallow waters based on the story of the Samaritan woman at the well (John 4). One of the young ladies in attendance felt she needed to share about an encounter she had many years ago.

My friend Katie is a flight attendant. She used to take yearly mission trips to Belize and said there was always something about what happened during those trips that caused strange sorts of things to happen when she returned to the states—strange, meaning good things. It was after one of her mission trips that she had the following encounter.

Katie was on a flight with an attendant she had never met before. Katie was wearing her wooden cross bracelet she had worn every day while in Belize. When she first got on her flight, she remembers seeing this new-to-her flight attendant named Julie and thinking Julie had it all together. She was thin and beautiful. As Katie and Julie chatted in the jump seats at takeoff, Katie learned Julie had a husband and three children. To Katie, it looked like Julie was living the dream. At the beginning of the flight, Katie mentioned she had recently returned from a mission trip to Belize. As sometimes happens, we fear what others think when we mention anything spiritual. Katie thought for sure Julie thought she was a "Bible-beater" as they went about their attendant duties.

Katie had the front part of the plane on the flight and Julie was assigned to the back part of the plane. Sometime into the long flight between DC and Dallas, Julie went up to the front and sat down next to Katie. There was a fierce desperation in her eyes Katie hadn't noticed before. Julie disclosed to Katie that at the beginning of the flight, a male passenger said to her, "You have a beautiful smile, but there is pain in it. Someone you know is hurting." Julie went on to tell Katie that even though her and her family attended church occasionally, they were really just going through the motions. Julie also mentioned she was involved with something she wanted and needed to get out of. Katie had somewhat of an idea what Julie was talking about, and she let Julie keep talking.

Julie told Katie she had recently prayed an "If you are real God, then help me get out of this" kind of prayer.

Katie, fully operating under the power of the Holy Spirit at this point, gently told Julie that if she truly wanted to stop doing what she was doing, she needed to turn around (repent), seek forgiveness from Jesus, and forgive herself. Katie then offered to pray for Julie. Right there in the front of the airplane, serious spiritual business took place. Some time after the flight, Julie confessed her indiscretion to her husband. He forgave her, and they are still together years later in a faith-filled marriage.

It all started when a man looked in Julie's eyes and saw the condition of her soul and spoke the words God needed her to hear that day. It continued with obedience by Katie to see that same desperation in Julie's eyes and to make the decision to care enough to invest the time. It wasn't necessarily convenient or comfortable, but it was a God-ordained moment for Katie to either participate in or refuse to be a part of. It saved Julie's marriage and family, and she is now actively interceding for the souls of spiritual orphans and all those needing prayer. By the way, the man the passenger mentioned as someone who was hurting, was Julie's husband. God's still in the miracle business today. Don't ever forget that.

It's a beautiful thing when the body of Christ operates in the gifts they have been given to bring heaven down to Earth.

———————

I recently learned something about the cornea in the eye. It is the eye's clear protective outer layer that admits light at the greatest angle. It makes up about two-thirds of the eye's optical power. The cornea's focusing power is fixed and can only be reshaped through a procedure that changes the geometry of the lens. It is the only organ in the body that does not require blood. Tears (and oxygen) do the work to keep eyes healthy. If the cornea were to get damaged by disease, infection, or injury, the resulting scars can affect your vision to varying degrees.

Spiritually speaking, some of our eyes have been scarred by whatever it is we have experienced or been taught. This blindness makes it hard for us to see people how God sees people. Perhaps these scars have made it hard for His light to penetrate our eyes when He is telling us to go one way or to help someone. The light we once had may be in danger of becoming darkness as we go spiritually blind to the need in front of and around us.

The people God is calling us to reach may also have deep wounds visible in their eyes. The eyes are the window to our souls. Scar tissue is hard to break, and it can't always be done right away. Helping someone with their scar tissue takes time, intentionality, and compassion.

The words God spoke to the prophet Ezekiel could be said today, "Son of man, you are living among a rebellious people. They have eyes to see but do not see and ears to hear but do not hear, for they are a rebellious people" (Ezek. 12:2). The people were rebellious because they had turned from God. God knew how rebellious their hearts were and that they weren't going to change their ways. He even told Ezekiel that the people were not going to listen to what Ezekiel prophesied, but God told Ezekiel to speak it anyway (Ezek. 3:7). God wasn't going to hold Ezekiel responsible for the sins of the people, but He would hold Ezekiel responsible for not delivering the message. It's interesting that God made a point of saying Ezekiel wasn't to go to a foreign people but to his own people. God said that if He had sent Ezekiel to a foreign people, they would have listened. That's how stubborn the rebellious Israelites were at the time (Ezek. 3:5–6).

In verse ten of chapter three, God told Ezekiel to listen carefully to the words He was giving to him and to "take them to heart." This is the same for you and me. We are not called to just go out and deliver a message; we are also called to take God's Word to heart. Ezekiel wept and petitioned for the people (Ezek. 11:13). The burden was so great. Do we have this great a burden for the destruction we see around us?

Advocating for the Spiritual Orphan

1. When you look in people's eyes, are you able to see their hurt, anger, or sadness? When you see it, what do you do about it?

2. When you are prompted by the Holy Spirit to speak a word of knowledge, do you do it? Why or why not? What pushes you forward or holds you back?

3. Have there been times in your life when you missed a ministry opportunity? Is there a way you can fix that today? Ask the Holy Spirit to bring that person or instance to mind. Think of ways

you can reach that person today if the Holy Spirit brings them to mind. Follow up with a call, a text, or a letter.

4. What do people see when they look in your eyes and witness your life? Are they attracted to you, or are they repelled? Ask around and see what others say about you. Be open to both the praise and the criticism.

Chapter Seven

IDENTIFY THE ENEMY

L OST PEOPLE ARE not the enemy. They are victims of the enemy."[33] Do you agree with this statement? What kind of thoughts come to mind when you think about the lost?

I agree 100 percent with this statement, however, I haven't always felt this way. You see, like many people, I was raised to believe that "bad people" were just that— bad people. I've been on the receiving end of some bad people's bad choices. It's not fun, and honestly, it is hard to feel empathy toward someone who hurts you or toward someone who generally just feels like a constant threat. But Jesus says we must. If Jesus left the comforts of heaven to come to Earth to save the lost, who are we to say no?

Jesus instructed people to love their enemies (Matt. 5:44). This was quite opposite of the thought process in the Old Testament when "an eye for an eye" was the cry of the day (Lev. 24:20). Today many people—both Christians and non-Christians alike—still believe the "eye for an eye" battle cry to be true. However, God is the One who loves His enemies best, because God has loved all of us with an everlasting love (Mal. 3:1). If He didn't love us, He would have given up on us a long time ago.

Throughout the Old Testament, people turned from God and their sinfulness was rampant. Think of the worst things you can think of. They were taking place even back then. Yet even in their wickedness, God offered love to the people who were His enemies. One such account is the well-known story of Jonah. We would be wise to learn a lesson from the prophet Jonah.

The people of Nineveh were cruel and sinful. They were enemies of God, but God desired for them to turn to Him. Jonah was a prophet in Israel during King Jeroboam II's reign. Jeroboam's reign was spiritually dark (like his father's), yet God allowed Jeroboam to continue the expansion started under Jeroboam's father, King Jehoash.

When God called Jonah to go to Nineveh and prophesy, the Assyrian empire was at a low point. While the Assyrians had at one time experienced dominance in the region, failed leadership and resistance from surrounding territories caused their dominance to lull. God needed the Assyrians to be at a place of need before they would be willing to listen to one of His chosen prophets. Can you see how even then, God got people's attention by placing them in a position of need?

Jonah had no interest whatsoever in talking with the Assyrians. Jonah did not have the heart of God for the spiritual orphan. Otherwise, he would have jumped at the opportunity to take the message of salvation and repentance into a wicked, pagan land. Jonah judged the

Assyrians and wanted to make sure he played no part in offering God's message of hope to the people of Nineveh.

I find it interesting that Jonah chose to run from God in his disobedience. Jonah could have stayed home, right? I mean, why did Jonah feel the need to jump on a ship and go completely in the opposite direction of where God was telling him to go? How outrageous is it that Jonah thought he could outrun God? Not only did Jonah run, but he hid. "But Jonah had gone below deck, where he lay down and fell into a deep sleep" (Jonah 1:5).

Why do we always try and hide from the Lord when we do something against His will?

———————

Remember Adam and Eve in the garden? They also hid after they had done something against God.

> Then the man and his wife heard the sound of the Lord God as he was walking in the garden in the cool of the day, and they hid from the Lord God among the trees of the garden. But the Lord God called to the man, "Where are you?" He answered, "I heard you in the garden, and I was afraid because I was naked; so I hid."
> —GENESIS 3:8–10

Prior to eating the forbidden fruit, Adam and Eve never knew nakedness. It was only when their eyes were opened to both good and evil did they see sin. Adam and Eve traded knowing God's goodness at all times for a piece of fruit dangling on a tree. Why would they do this? They did it because the serpent tricked them.

As soon as they took a bite of the forbidden fruit, their eyes were immediately opened and they recognized their nakedness (Gen. 3:7). Nakedness in the Bible refers to sin. It is in our most vulnerable state that we recognize our depravity. Whether it is our own sin or the sin of others, sin often makes us run from God instead of to God. I think it's because inherently at our core we know the holiness of God whether we admit He is our God or not.

God dealt harshly with Adam and Eve because of their sin. He banished them from the garden and told them they would have to work a hard land until the day they died. Why was banishment necessary? The banishment was necessary because the Garden of Eden represented the place in which God walked among His creation. It represents for us today a picture of what heaven will be like. Since Adam and Eve ate the forbidden fruit, they became like God knowing both good and evil. And like God, as well as the other two persons of the Trinity (Jesus and the Holy Spirit), Adam and Eve would live forever in the garden. Sounds great, right? Not exactly.

When Adam and Eve ate the fruit, their eyes were opened to evil. If God allowed them to stay in the garden, Adam and Eve would have lived forever in a fallen state. God never intended for His creation to be broken. He wants it whole. As early as this Genesis account, God provided a way of escape for the people He created.

In His mercy, God stationed mighty cherubim to the east of the garden along with a flaming sword that flashed back and forth to guard the way to the tree of life (Gen. 3:24). God stationed the cherubim to the east because, as mentioned before, moving east represents leaving the presence or blessings of God, judgment, or estrangement. The cherubim guarded the place in which Adam and Eve left the garden, and the flaming sword highlighted the only way to eternal life for mankind.

God's plan from the beginning was straightforward. He wanted to be in harmony with His creation. However, God's creation messed it up. It started first with the angel Lucifer and then continued with Eve, Adam, and everyone since then. However, even in that moment when God said to Adam, "Who told you that you were naked?" (Gen. 3:11), God had compassion in His voice. Can you feel the pain in God's voice when He asked Eve, "What *have* you done?" (Gen. 3:13, emphasis added)?

I don't think God was looking for a confession at this point. I think God was painfully verbalizing all that would come because of this one poor decision.

The fruit of that forbidden tree allowed Adam and Eve to see both good and evil. They saw the goodness of God (He didn't strike them dead that day), and they also saw evil. Evil was that slippery little snake who deceived Eve. The deceiver was identified. His name would be told for generations and eventually his name would make it into the written Word. However, for some reason we forget who our enemy is. Our enemy wasn't Eve, Adam, or even God that day (despite the fact we are still suffering the consequences of their bad choice). Our enemy was and will always be Satan.

If we continue to identify people as our enemies instead of Satan, we waste our energy and time fighting the wrong enemy. As New Testament believers, God hasn't given us instruction to fight our enemies; He gave us instruction to love people. The Old Testament is filled with accounts of God giving very specific instructions for His chosen people to take land and to drive out the enemies of God. However, in the New Testament we see none of this. God has provided an instrument of peace and hope in the Person of Jesus Christ. The moment the gospel went forth to the Gentiles, the doors of heaven were open to all people. The only people who are enemies of God these days are spiritual orphans, the people who do not believe in Jesus Christ as their Savior.

As Christ followers, we are not commanded to kill, judge, speak ill of, condemn, or change God's enemies. We are commanded to love them and show them Christ's love. We are to tell the stories of His amazing grace and share about the free gift of salvation God is offering to the nations. Why the God of the universe would choose to use us is beyond me but He has, and time is short.

A few years ago, a picture circulated in the news that captivated me. You can google the spectacular image NASA's Chandra X-ray Observatory recorded some seventeen thousand light years away (one light year equals approximately six trillion miles)![34] At the center of this nebula is a pulsar whose spewed energy is creating intriguing structures. One of the structures has been named the "Hand of

God" by NASA. How often do you see science and religion overlap these days?

Some may call this image an optical illusion due to all the light being infused by the atmosphere and the exploding stars. However, one thing is certain, each section of the picture is a different piece to the puzzle within this nebula. Another thing is certain is that it doesn't matter if the picture is an optical illusion because God is the God of creation (including light), and ultimately He controls all that takes place here on Earth and in heaven.

What is so fascinating about this photo and the fact that science merges with religion? It is scriptural. God told us from the beginning that He is the One who created day and night and the sun and stars.

> And God said, "Let there be lights in the expanse of the heavens to separate the day from the night. And let them be for signs and for seasons, and for days and years, and let them be lights in the expanse of the heavens to give light upon the earth." And it was so. And God made the two great lights—the greater light to rule the day and the lesser light to rule the night—and the stars. And God set them in the expanse of the heavens to give light on the earth, to rule over the day and over the night, and to separate the light from the darkness. And God saw that it was good. And there was evening and there was morning, the fourth day.
>
> —GENESIS 1:14–19

The prophet Joel also said that the Lord "will show wonders in the heavens and on the earth, blood and fire and columns of smoke" (Joel 2:30). Peter referenced the prophet Joel's words in his first act of public preaching on the day of Pentecost in Acts 2. Jesus said in Luke 21:25, "There will be strange signs in the sun, moon and stars. And here on earth nations will be in turmoil, perplexed by the roaring seas and strange tides."

Excuse me while I clear my throat.

I know people have been predicting the return of Jesus for many years. The apostles spoke of His return being at any moment. We've anxiously held our breath during the threat of nuclear war, global warming, the threat of World War III, Y2K, and the Mayan calendar. However, as Christians we must not negate all things having to do with "signs and wonders." Jesus said in Mark 13:31–37:

> Heaven and earth will pass away, but my words will not pass away. But concerning that day or that hour, no one knows, not even the angels in heaven, nor the Son, but only the Father. Be on guard, keep awake. For you do not know when the time will come. It is like a man going on a journey, when he leaves home and puts his servants in charge, each with his work, and commands the doorkeeper to stay awake. Therefore, stay awake—for you do not know when the master of the house will come, in the evening, or at midnight, or when the rooster crows, or in the morning—lest he come suddenly and find you asleep. And what I say to you I say to all: Stay awake.
>
> —NLT

When I first saw the picture, the hand looked like it was reaching down into a ball of fire. However, I then read that it appeared the hand is closing into a fist. The hand looks so real it looks as though it has fingernails.[35] In the Genesis account, it says, "God created human beings in his own image" (Gen. 1:27). Our image is His image. How scary it is that it looks like the hand is closing. NASA describes the hand being separate from the red lights. To me, the red lights look like the fiery pits of hell, full of brimstone and heat.

The first time I saw the picture, the Spirit said to me, "My hand is plucking people from the fiery pits of hell one at a time." However, the closing fist made the hair on the back of my neck stand up and Holy Spirit goosebumps shoot down my body, as I heard Him say, "But the time will come when My Hand will close, and I will pluck no more!"

I was so taken by these thoughts and the picture that I tried to share my enthusiasm with my family. My then six-year-old was intrigued. I started talking about the picture and the message and he got quiet—real quiet. Then he asked, "Am I going to be OK when Jesus comes back? What about you, daddy, Spenser, and Grace?"

The whole concept scared the pants off him, and he was afraid to go into the playroom right after that! He's OK now, and I assured him that, yes, the five of us have secured our place in heaven with Jesus because we have confessed Him as our Lord and Savior.

If you have time, research the "Hand of God" image on your own and see what the Spirit says to you. Does the fact Jesus could return at any moment concern you? Is your salvation on the right side of the cross? What about the people you love? The people you work with? The family across the street? The stranger working behind the counter? Time is of the essence.

God has asked us not to spend our time judging and condemning. He hasn't asked us to present Him with ideas on how to fix the world. He wants us to share about His gift of grace with the people He created. While they are His enemies prior to salvation, He loves them nevertheless. He wants them to become His adopted children (no longer spiritual orphans) at the moment of their salvation. Will you be the one to deliver this great message to spiritual orphans regardless of their current choice of lifestyle, sin level, or location?

God chose Jonah to be His vessel. However, Jonah wanted personal safety and security over missional living. He feared the wicked people of Nineveh. He wanted to hold onto his God, but not share his God with people who desperately needed God. He wanted to be in control of deciding who was and wasn't worthy enough for God to save. Even though the Assyrian's power was at an all-time low, they had a track record of wickedness. God had a plan to reveal His glory not only to an unlikely people group but also to a people who had become comfortable in their wicked living and their allegiance to nationalism rather than to God. If a prophet of God did not understand the heart of God, how was God's love to be displayed to the world? Yikes! How many of us today have Jonah hearts instead of Jesus hearts?

God calls us to love our enemies so that we may be children of our Father in heaven (Matt. 5:44–45). The way in which we live out love demonstrates our love and respect for our Father. I don't know about you, but I know that when my children think about how their actions might impact my reputation, it shows me how much or how little they respect me, or how much more they still need to mature in their understanding of who I am to them.

The same can be said of our relationship with God. When we choose to love others well, we are choosing to sacrifice and be OK with being uncomfortable. However, when we choose to not love well, we tell God that our wants, needs, and comfort level are much more important than our being good stewards of the love He has shown for us. If God loves the people in this world, shouldn't we love them too?

Jonah didn't love well. He ran. He almost allowed his own feelings and emotions to get in the way of sparing lives from complete destruction. What if God hadn't sent the storm and the great fish? What if the story ended with Jonah permanently moving to Tarshish and the local newspaper headline read, "Assyrian Empire Destroyed Because One Man Said No to God!" I don't know about you, but I would not want to be the man or woman who had that weighing on me for all my days and into eternity. But do you know what? This headline could be said of most of us any given day of the week if we are not careful. Why? Because every single day God is asking us to be faithful and obedient and to love others well. Every day, God puts people in our path who need to hear about Jesus and their need for Him because today might very well be their last day on Earth or the moment in history when a life-altering decision is made.

Prior to sending Jonah, God had never sent a prophet out to a pagan land. Prophets were used only to deliver messages to the chosen people of Israel. However, this time God was doing a new thing. God told Jonah to announce His judgment against the people of Nineveh (Jonah 1:1–2). God wasn't asking Jonah to give them an "out" clause. He was only asking Jonah to deliver a message of judgment. A self-righteous person would love nothing more than this, right? But for some reason, Jonah didn't want to go to Nineveh.

God was sending a person who personally received messages from God to a people group who was anything but God-fearing. The one who was called to be the mouthpiece for God ran from God while those wicked Assyrians who didn't follow God ended up running to God. I am always amazed when the Holy Spirit uses something that happened more than two thousand years ago to bring conviction.

It took Jonah fearing for his life before he agreed to do what God asked him to do. God threw Jonah into the danger and chaos of the sea to give him time to consider his options. I can relate.

I was so fearful before I surrendered to Jesus. I was fearful because I didn't personally know the Savior—the One who protects me, prays for me, and loves me. I battled an unseen, unidentified enemy who wanted to end my life. I feared death. And it turns out, it wasn't a physical death I was fearing but a spiritual one. I was a self-identified Christian who was an enemy of God. I had never put my trust and faith in Jesus as my own personal Lord and Savior. I totally knew who God was, but I had no idea about the gospel message. However, in the same way God spared Jonah, God spared me.

I spent several years floundering, struggling, and sinning because I ran from God. Looking back, I wish more people would have been concerned with my soul. I was making my way through life in a spiritually dead wasteland. I know now that the gospel was close to me because I know churches and Christians who live in the areas where I walked and lived. These same churches operated during my spiritual orphan years. Yet, somehow none of those Christians ever delivered the message to me. I wonder if they were asked by God but didn't respond or obey. I certainly know I had seasons of desperation during those years where my sinful heart would have been open to hearing about grace and love.

It's easy to be cynical in today's world, but we need to work hard against allowing ourselves to be too hardened to help people. A couple of years ago, we helped someone who was literally at death's door because of drug addiction.

Sadly, most might have written him off. Helping people with addictions or problems is messy, unpredictable, and often frustrating. My husband didn't write this guy off. If you know my husband, you know how generous he is. He paid legal fees and bail fees for this someone. We helped him medically kick his addiction. This guy had to do the spiritual work with God alone, and he did. God saved this man from death, gave him a good-paying job, and reunited him with his wife (from whom he had been divorced) and child.

Without our asking (and without our expecting), he began to send us checks every month to pay off his debt. Every month when I open the envelope, I think of his honor in doing this and how great God is. Without God, it was impossible but with God, it was possible.

For all those still waiting on something or someone, don't allow the waiting to get you so cynical that you don't help the next person or engage with God.

After Jonah was thrown ashore by the big fish, he appeared in the city a complete mess. You can imagine what Jonah must have looked like after spending three long days in the belly of a great fish.

We must remember, rebellion to God causes a person to be a spiritual orphan. This rebellion includes the denial of God and resistance to surrendering to Jesus. However, it is God's mercy that allows a person to be His child if they seek Him with sincere and repentant hearts. If we truly understand the depths of our own rebellion, we will be better able to serve those in the throes of rebellion. If we believe we've never sinned (or sinned greatly), it will be reflected in the way we treat those separated from the Father.

Choices make people spiritual orphans, but He doesn't want to leave them as orphans. He wants to call them sons and daughters. If He loves them even in their rebellion, so should we. If we fail to love, we are enacting our own rebellion toward God just like Jonah did when he refused to go to Nineveh.

Over five years ago, a friend of ours planted Awaken Church in Charleston, South Carolina. Brandon Bowers, the lead pastor, started the church by reaching out to the community. He didn't just hang a sign on a building, open the doors, and expect everyone to come in. No, he started his church relationally. He always reaches out to people, and after one visit to Awaken, you would see that he is training his leaders to reach people in the same way. This not only influences the members, but it also affects the guests.

In July of 2015, a man by the name of Paul attended Awaken Church for the first time. At the time, Paul was a man fully engrossed in the homosexual lifestyle. As a young child, he had been bullied and called feminine names by other children and his step-mother. As a teenager, he was molested by his step-grandfather. He eventually began to watch pornography as a teenager and at the age of seventeen, he gave in to what everyone said he was.

From that moment on, everything about him revolved around being gay.

At the age of twenty, he tried ecstasy for the first time, and eventually became hooked on even harder drugs. The drugs for him were an escape from all that had happened to him and all he was taking part in. As a side note, sometimes we see people using drugs and think drugs are the problem when in fact a lot of them are using drugs to cover up deeper issues. We can't just look at the drugs as the problem, we need to look at what is going on inside the person.

Paul ended up at Awaken that July day through an invite. When he walked into the church, he was warmly greeted by almost a half-dozen people. That stuck with him. The church didn't reject him because he was gay. They didn't not talk to him. They didn't tell him to leave. And you know what, he wanted to come back the next week. I know this sounds like a no-brainer, but believe me, it isn't.

Not every church would have handled Paul's situation in the same way. Just a few weeks ago, a friend visited a new church near where we live and in less than ten minutes, church members were berating her because she was a single mom without even knowing all the facts. Sadly, not every church has arrived and not every church loves all people well. Bob Goff's recent Instagram post read, "Don't be mean; it makes mean people look normal."[36]

Let's not make mean, unkind, and unwelcoming look normal in the church. Jesus isn't mean; He is love. Let's look more like Jesus.

Paul made it back to church the next Sunday, and the following day, he had lunch with one of the pastors. During the lunch, Paul described how God basically told him that He didn't make him the way everyone said he was. The pastor didn't know what to say because he thought the conversation was going to go in an entirely different direction. Paul knew he wasn't created to be gay. A couple weeks later, he was baptized at the church.

Five months later, Paul began leading a community group and a few months after that, he was asked to help launch another campus for the church. What could have ended disastrously for Paul, instead turned out to be a beautiful picture of God's redemption and love for the spiritual orphan.

Satan worked his evil through people who were supposed to care for Paul. They failed him, but God in His goodness rescued Paul as Paul cried out to God in prayer. Paul became part of God's family when he fully surrendered his life to Christ. He also became part of a church family who spoke life into him instead of deceit and lies and walked beside him as he figured out his new lifestyle.

In speaking with Paul recently about this book, he informed me that he was about to ask his girlfriend to marry him in a few hours. He met the girl who would become his girlfriend the very first night of his very first small group at Awaken. God and God's people really are amazing. When we let God be God and when we act like Jesus told us to, miracles will happen. Lives are rescued and changed for His glory.

By the way, Paul's girlfriend said, "Yes!"

Sometimes in our desire to share the love of Christ with people and the truths found in the Bible, we come across as judgmental and harsh instead of concerned and caring. I know I have in the past. Not every conversation or situation is going to be as quick and neat as Paul's, but that doesn't mean we shouldn't or can't do our part.

During a recent afternoon snack date with my youngest child, he said, "Did you hear what happened to dad?"

My first thought was he got another speeding ticket. Thankfully, that wasn't it.

My son said, "Dad was at a coffee shop downtown this morning, and the barista kept looking at the bracelet he was wearing." My husband wears an "I Am Second"[37] bracelet most every day. I Am Second is a Christian organization. On several occasions, the barista mentioned "her wife."

Now, we aren't sure whether she was really excited about her wife, or whether she was trying to instigate an argument with my husband about his view on gay marriage. Either way, my husband didn't give in to her. Instead, he treated her with kindness and left her a large tip. That left a really confused look on her face.

We don't know the conversations people may be having with God behind the scenes. We don't know how God is moving in people's hearts because we aren't God. God doesn't ask us to do the heavy lifting; He can handle that. He just asks us to love people by showing love. Paul told the Ephesians to only say things that are good and helpful to encourage people and he warned them not to grieve the Holy Spirit (Eph. 4:29–30).

Jonah threw a fit because God chose to save the wicked people of Nineveh. Some of us today are throwing our own mini temper tantrums because God is asking us to reach into parts of society we don't want to because we don't think they deserve a place in the kingdom. Jonah's attitude and actions placed him in the belly of a great fish and on a hill without shade in the scorching heat.

Jonah's consequences for running from God's instruction should be a warning to us all that God is serious about the call to reach the nations and to love people. Jonah took his eyes off God and put them on himself and his own personal views. He wished death where God said there would be life. Don't be like Jonah. Keep your eyes on His plan that all would be brought unto salvation and be called children of God. The more we do this, the better things will be. The less spiritual orphans we have walking this Earth, the better.

Advocating for the Spiritual Orphan

1. Whom do you see as your enemy? List them by name.

2. Whom does God see as His enemy? List them by name.

3. If God told you to go into a hostile environment, would you react the same as Jonah or would you respond differently?

4. Do you often feel like you are the only righteous one living amongst wickedness? How can you help those living apart from God find God? What message is God asking you to share with people? Are you sharing it?

5. If you knew Jesus was returning today, would you be sad about those who don't know Jesus or would you think it was their fault they haven't listened?

Chapter Eight

FOCUS ON ETERNAL THINGS

W E HAVE RULES and laws in place to protect us. The law wasn't sent to condemn the righteous but to help the unrighteous get and stay on the right path. Without any boundaries for wrongdoing, we have no idea what is right and what is wrong.

Laws can also divide people. Those who abide by the law are considered law-abiding citizens, and those who break the law are considered criminals. Law-abiding citizens inherently have a dislike, distrust of, and often a disgust toward criminals. They are much like David as he cried out to God on many occasions for help from his enemies who were out to get him and harm him. He called them evil-doers and asked God to expedite judgment upon those wicked people.

> Turn from evil and do good; then you will dwell in the land forever. For the Lord loves the just and will not forsake his faithful ones.
>
> —PSALM 37:27–28

As New Testament believers, we live under the covenant of grace instead of constraint under the Mosaic Law.

I, for one, am so grateful for grace. Spend a little time in Leviticus and you can see how difficult it must have been for people before the resurrection of Jesus Christ. Any day and at any moment, any number of the many laws could be broken. Then there was a long list of sacrifices that needed to be offered and remedies taken to get the person back in right standing. On many occasions, God offered no opportunity for repentance or sacrifices but instead enacted judgment instantly.

The thing about grace is that it models for us what we need to live out. Grace upon grace. It isn't easy to breathe out grace to people who are different, but extending grace is exactly what Jesus does over and over again. When Jesus looks at people, He looks directly into their hearts. He knows their thoughts. Grace is even harder to extend to those who live wildly unrighteous lives. Those people who don't fit into neat boxes or within the bounds of the law (both federal and state laws as well as those laws from the Old Testament we like to pull out from time to time when handy) present a challenge for most Christians to live out Jesus's command to love others. But we must. We must be more concerned with the eternal than the here and now. If someone looks too far gone that is exactly the time they need to feel and witness love the most.

As Jesus hung upon the cross on April 3, 33 AD, he hung between two criminals. Both criminals initially mocked Jesus, however right before his death, one of the criminals turned his life over to Jesus.

Jesus, the pure and sinless Son of God hung between two criminals who were so bad they were killed by crucifixion. Despite their past, Jesus said to the criminal who accepted Him as Savior, "Truly I tell you, today you will be with me in paradise" (Luke 23:43). There wasn't an opportunity for the criminal to change his life or do a discipleship program with anyone. He couldn't prove whether his salvation experience was for real or not. He couldn't personally share his testimony with anyone because, well, it was too late. He had a few minutes left to live. Jesus didn't care the man had been a criminal. Jesus was only concerned about the man's eternity. We must care about the spiritual orphan's eternity too.

Childhood sexual abuse is a topic that is near and dear to my heart. However, there is a slight twist to what I am about to say. I am prepared for the naysayers, the rolling eyes, and the "are you kidding me's?" but please hear me out.

Years ago during the same weekend, I heard two different pastors at my church preach on Luke 5:12–26. Both pastors started out their sermons by clarifying what it meant to have leprosy back in Jesus's time. They explained what a person had to do if they woke up with a problem with their skin, what happened if the high priest suspected leprosy (be banished by themselves outside the city limits for a week with no human contact), be reexamined by the high priest after that time, and if leprosy was the diagnosis, they banished the person into the leper colony for as long as it persisted. The lepers lived in complete isolation from their loved ones, they couldn't bathe, and on top of all of that, they stunk. As my pastors quoted, "They were living, walking dead men." Could you imagine?

Shortly after hearing these two messages, the Lord laid childhood sexual abuse on my heart. However, the Lord brought me to a different side of the issue based primarily on the passage of the leper in Luke 5:12–16. During that week, I came across an article on the Christian Post website entitled "Church Conducts 'Adults Only' Services for Sex Offenders, Others."[38] At first, I thought to myself, "Eww, I would *never* step foot in that service."

Yes, I know, very Christian of me.

As I read the article, I was shocked to discover that sex offenders are today's living, walking dead men (and women). The article reminded me that as a registered sex offender, a person can't and shouldn't be around children for legal and therapeutic reasons. While that makes sense, have you ever thought about the fact that a registered sex offender can't attend church because children may be present? I can honestly say that thought had never once crossed my mind. Even as perverted as their crimes are, a registered sex offender who has served his prison time cannot go to God's house during a regular worship service.

Wow.

Registered sex offenders are the ones who are forever required to announce to the world the crime(s) they committed. They must yell, "Unclean, unclean," even if the Lord has made them clean. While I understand that felons must also disclose their criminal record at times, it is not made available to the general public. If my neighbor across the street murdered a child but did not sexually abuse a child, I would not know that information. I could be sitting near a murderer, tax evader, or thief any given Sunday and not even know it. However, sex offenders wear a scarlet letter forever. It starts early on during their prison time. Upon entrance to prison, a sex offender is given a unique numbering system so the entire prison population (not just the guards) knows they are a sex offender. Sex offenders are not treated very well in prison. There is no wonder the suicide rate among them is extremely high. I did criminal defense legal work for a few years and saw the results of what happened to our sex offender clients firsthand.

Whatever punishment they receive is a consequence of the choice they made by violating the law, and the sentence is justified by the law. However, what I have been thinking about is that even if a sex offender has repented of his sins, God has forgiven him, and he has served his prison time, he cannot be wholly integrated back into society. No modern-day high priest can call him clean; psychiatrists can't fill this role.

Don't get me wrong. I am not suggesting we allow sex offenders unlimited access to children. I am human (and an abuse survivor), and I have strong emotions about protecting innocent children. I am also a mother who never wants her children to suffer this kind of abuse by an adult. But at the same time, how can I ignore the fact these people are the only class of people in the US who can't choose to attend church? The need for the church service referenced in the article came out of the church's prison ministry. How can we truly rehabilitate these sex offenders if we alienate them from the opportunity to corporately worship God (and hear the gospel presented) for the remainder of their lives on Earth?

This is a unique need we need to address for many reasons. While sex offenders appear to be monsters to most of the world, they are just one example of how Satan ensnares people in his web. Many of these offenders were themselves victims of childhood sexual abuse or exposed to sexually deviant behavior as children. Satan planted this perverted seed early on, and Satan's seeds tend to grow wild and out of control if given the opportunity.

Childhood sexual abuse is a real problem. The numbers are high, but likely much higher than we even know because, often, the abuse goes unreported. It is estimated that in the US alone, approximately three million children are sexually abused every year—about one every ten seconds. In the few minutes it takes you to read this, at least thirty children will be sexually abused in the US. The numbers are even worse abroad. The scary fact is that one in three girls and one in five boys will be sexually abused before the age of eighteen.[39]

Do these numbers make your stomach queasy? They do mine. They also sometimes keep me up at night. I love my children and would give my own life for theirs. This kind of abuse is a real and present danger both within the church and outside of the church.

I pray that Christians awaken to the needs of people who have suffered sexual abuse as well as those who have been the perpetrators of sexual abuse. Therapy is great, but the pain associated with abuse causes many to stumble and fall later in life. Addiction, future abusive relationships, risky behaviors, divorce, trust issues, and homelessness are just a few of the examples of what happens to people who can't get out from under the pain and sorrow of abuse. We must provide a safety net for those who have suffered abuse and those who have abused. Healing needs to take place. People are not called to judge—that is God's job. We have cancer centers to treat cancer with medicine. We have spine institutes to treat back problems with medicine. However, sexual abuse can't be treated with medicine (except maybe castration and that's extreme). It gets into the soul and soul issues must be dealt with through the Word and by His people utilizing the full power of the One who heals hearts and souls.

Whom do we love more? The victim or the perpetrator? Whom do you think Jesus loves?

The leper in Luke 5 took a great risk and broke many laws to get to Jesus. He said, "Lord, if you are willing, you can heal me and make me clean" (v. 12). Jesus then did something that was unheard of at that time—He reached out His hand and touched the leper. Jesus was willing to heal the leper and so He did. Sick people need Jesus, and we need to not limit access to Jesus because of people's sin or our personal preferences.

Sex offenders are a part of society we do not want to reach out to or touch. I honestly never thought I would be saying something like

> *We do what we do because of who or what we love. Love decides.*[40]
>
> —ANN VOSKAMP

137

this, but for so many reasons, we do need to reach out to them. We need to help them resist committing future sins and crimes, we need to help them resist wanting to harm themselves, and we need to make sure they can get to Jesus for healing, as well as worship with other believers. I know going to church does not make one saved, but biblical community is so important for growth and accountability.

What would you do if someone said you could never attend church again because of a sin you committed? This is exactly what sex offenders experience. No other criminals suffer this same fate once they leave prison. What would Jesus say? What would He want us to say and do?

> What causes division, strife, and misery among men is not race, culture, language, or class but sin and rebellion.[11]
>
> —FREDDIE GARCIA

Sin is sin no matter how we categorize it, but the sin that matters most is intentionally denying God and refusing to accept Jesus Christ as Savior. This also includes blaspheming the Holy Spirit (Mark 3:29). The consequence of this sin is eternal death. But what about those who don't know they are sinning against the Trinity? Jesus not only had something to say about the person committing this type of sin; He also had something to say to the forgiven person.

Jesus often taught in parables. It was His way of

speaking truth without overtly speaking the truth or calling out specific individuals. He would speak in parables, and the Holy Spirit would reveal bits and pieces of what Jesus was saying to whom it needed to be revealed. In one particular parable about the Lord's coming, Jesus spoke of a master who was absent from his home for a period of time and the servant's actions while the master was away (Luke 12:35–48).

In the parable, Jesus said that the servant who knew exactly what was expected of him should do what was right while the master was away and be ready for the master's return. Jesus said some would choose to do other things—wrong things—and lose the trust of the master resulting in severe punishment. However, Jesus said the servant who didn't know but did something wrong would be punished lightly (Luke 12:48). In a twist, Jesus said a more severe punishment would be levied upon the one who knew as opposed to the one who didn't know. Some may say this isn't fair. I tend to think this is a good example of a prodigal (someone who knows better) versus a spiritual orphan (someone who has no clue).

The ones who are saved and working unto the Lord have a higher responsibility upon their lives than those who are still wandering and lost in this world. Jesus said so. Lost people don't always know they are lost, and until we stop treating the lost as if they know they are acting outside the will of God when they don't even know God, our judgmental attitudes toward them will only push them further and further from Christ. For some unknown reason, God entrusts people to be messengers of the gospel.

His lost children include the "much" believers have been entrusted to reach and care for in Luke 12:48. God loves His "much" so greatly that He sent His only Son for all the world (John 3:16).

We hold the lost and unconverted to a biblical standard they know nothing about while at the same time violating the biblical standard we should know all about. Jesus held nothing back when He reached the lost. Nothing. He wasn't afraid of what people thought or the standard customs of the day, and He didn't care whether people would respond positively to the hope He extended. He loved anyway. The One who is the Word spoke the Word to all, never holding back from anyone. The ones who responded were often those with childlike faith. They were the ones who knew their lack and need and knew the One who stood before them who read their mail as He read their hearts.

Oh, if we all could be more like Jesus who focused on all the right things—eternal things and matters of the heart.

During His final farewell, Jesus gave the disciples a new commandment, "Love one another. As I have loved you, so you must love one another" (John 13:34). What would this love do? Jesus said that if they loved each other, it would prove to the world they were His disciples (John 13:35). Jesus didn't tell them right away to go out and love everyone. He started with their small circle. He said to the eleven still gathered around the table, "Love each other."

If we can get love right within our small circles first, we have a much better chance of living love everywhere we go. Jesus's love was apparent everywhere He went because He is love (1 John 4:8). He loved the disciples as much as any sinner or sick person He came across. He even loved all the religious leaders who wanted Him dead. The miracles Jesus performed might have been the reason some initially followed, but it was His love that caused people to stick around. When you are with someone who has that much love for people, it is hard to stay away.

For Noah's wicked generation, God sent a boat. A boat is but a vessel made of wood with no ability to love. For our generation, God sent a person bursting with love. Jesus came from God the Father in heaven who has a love we can't even begin to fathom.

God loved the world—this broken, sinful, dirty, and disobedient world—so much that He sent Jesus to save the world He created. No other prophet or king before Jesus could express this kind of love. Only Jesus could, and the crazy thing is, Jesus said that every single follower of Christ could and should love people the way He loves people. Do we utilize this amazing miracle to its fullest potential?

———

Every once in a while, I find myself thinking a series of what-ifs? What if Jesus hadn't radically transformed my life and sent people into my husband's and my life to help us and disciple us? Where would we be now?

Do you ever have these thoughts? I talked earlier about remembering where you came from, but we also need to focus on where we are going and why we are going there. Jesus said, "But seek first his kingdom and his righteousness, and then..." (Matt. 6:33). We need to start every day seeking God's will first.

Very few things in life stand out as mile markers—you know, those moments in life where you see a fork in the road so clearly and as you look back at that exact moment, you realize God was there before the fork in the road, at the fork in the road, and with you on the chosen road.

For us, as a family, one of our mile markers is a man by the name of Mike Fechner. Matthew 6:33 was his life verse. In everything he did, he sought the kingdom of God first. He laid down his life for others—especially for those people who many would never take an interest in. Although Mike was from a predominantly white suburb and at one time a pastor on staff at a predominantly upper-middle class white church, Mike felt a burden for the people in the inner city. These were his people.

Mike knew what it felt like to not feel welcomed. During his high school years, Mike's father was stationed in Hawaii. While that sounds like a dream opportunity for most of us, it was a place and a time in his life where he experienced racial hatred. The locals called him a *haole*. Hawaiians use the term *haole* to refer to white people and usually in a disparaging manner.[41] God can and will use our pain and life experiences if we allow Him to, and God did exactly that with Mike. Mike knew the only thing that could truly bring people together was love. The color of our skin or our nationality shouldn't separate us or cause us to hate one another. Mike was determined to love as many people as he could for as long as he could.

Solely by a God-ordained appointment, my husband

met Mike several years ago. Their first meeting took place shortly after Mike was diagnosed with stage four nonsmoker's lung cancer. At the time of his diagnosis, the doctors gave him eighteen months to live (he ended up walking this earth for a little over five years after that first diagnosis). That God-ordained meeting led us to eventually see Mike share his testimony at the church where he was a former staff pastor.

That one meeting changed the trajectory and legacy of our family forever. Wherever my testimony is shared for all my days, Mike's name will be a part of it. His legacy of faith, endurance, perseverance, suffering, and taking up his cross daily will live on long past my days.

Mike's life and legacy shifted the kingdom of darkness into light. Not because Mike was Mike, but because he was willing to be broken, bruised, battered, and serve out of complete obedience and surrender to the Lord. We should all live with this mind-set. We should be more consumed with pushing back the kingdom of darkness and ushering the lost into the kingdom of God. I know without a doubt Mike was ushered into the presence of God with the words, "Well done good and faithful servant," because he sought the kingdom of God first.

Mike was a spiritual mentor to my husband, and

> *Because you are not witnessing, many have not heard the Gospel. They will be eternally separated from God. What a consequence of our apathy! It is time for us to put feet to our faith.*[43]
>
> —WATCHMAN NEE

Mike was a spiritual mentor to many others as well. He was the kind of guy who would give the shirt off his back for someone in need, regardless of their age, color, or life situation. There isn't a day that goes by that someone I know doesn't mention Mike's name. He was that kind of a guy.

But you know what? We all can be that kind of person. We can all love better. We can all love differently. If we seek first the kingdom of God, we'll know in our hearts there is room for everyone in His kingdom. Jesus said, "Make every effort to enter through the narrow door, because many, I tell you, will try to enter and will not be able to" (Luke 13:24). Right after saying this, Jesus said the door wouldn't be open for very long. Eventually, the Master is going to close the door.

The sad reality is that many people won't ever enter the gates of heaven. They will be banished into the abyss of hell and long-suffering. It's not their fault completely. Maybe it is our fault. Maybe we aren't sharing the gospel enough. Maybe we don't love people consistently enough. Maybe we say we are Christians, but then we post or repost ugly social media comments. Sometimes what we are feeling shouldn't be made public. It should be taken directly to the One who can reconcile and cleanse our hearts before we think it's the other person who needs the cleaning.

Did you understand what Watchman Nee said in his statement? He said that people would be eternally separated from God because of our apathy. He didn't say it was because of God's anger or judgment. He said it was because of us—Christians—who fail to do the work for any number of reasons. The verse I cling to for my ministry is Isaiah 52:7. It says, "How beautiful on the mountains are the feet of those who bring good news." The phrase *good news* in this verse refers to the gospel. I want to see mountains filled with beautiful feet bringing the good news to the lost, the suffering, the hurting, the unaware, the prisoners, and even some church-goers who haven't yet received the good news for themselves.

The crazy thing about God is that He chooses to use humans to be the carriers of the good news. I'll never understand why. Jesus's thoughts were always and will always be on eternal things and so must ours. If we choose lives of comfort over compassion, there will be consequences. People will die without reconciliation with their Father. They will die as spiritual orphans even though the Father desperately wanted to adopt them into His forever family.

We are never responsible for the outcome; we are only responsible for our obedience. We can't force or coerce someone into accepting Jesus as their Lord and Savior. But God knows exactly who He is drawing to Himself through Jesus (John 6:44). The battle is always the Lord's. He does the choosing. He knows exactly what is going on and nothing catches Him by surprise. When it looks like things are completely out of control, know that He is sovereign over all of it. And most importantly, He loves His creation and every created thing (Ps. 33:5). He wants nothing more than to have every single person adopted into His family and with Him for all of eternity. God wants people to fear Him so that they can rely on His unfailing love and so He can rescue them from death (Ps. 33:18–19).

We must see every person who comes into our lives, and even those who come across our screens, as an opportunity for adoption into God's family. We can't see them as God's children unless they have been adopted through their belief in Jesus. To blindly believe that we are all God's children is to not know God's heart or God's Word. If everyone ever born was a child of God, there would have never been a reason for war, famine, or for Jesus to step out of heaven. If the Holy Spirit nudges you to speak, speak. If the Holy Spirit nudges you to smile, smile. If the Holy Spirit nudges you to pray, pray. Eternity is at stake, and the stakes are high. Don't ever be ashamed of the gospel of Jesus Christ (Rom. 1:16), and don't ever be ashamed to be a messenger of the gospel. You hold the key to life in your heart. Offer this key to others as much as you can, for as long as you can, for as many days as you can through whatever gifts, talents, and opportunities God provides.

My friend recently said, "Do you want to be remembered for the title you hold or the things you accumulate, or do you want to be remembered through people's testimonies of how you impacted their lives and made a difference in their walk with Jesus?" Impacting lives and making a difference takes time and effort. But most importantly it takes a heart that wants to be a part of changing someone's forever story. It can be hard, frustrating, and sometimes even a little dangerous. We can learn a thing or two from a courageous queen named Esther.

In the Book of Esther, we are told about Esther, a physical orphan (Esther 2:7). She was raised by her cousin, Mordecai. She resided in Persia because her family was a part of the *diaspora* ("scattering")—the Jews who were scattered during the exile. For some reason, her family had not returned to Judah. Perhaps this was an indication of comfort in a foreign land because of Mordecai's position within the Persian government.

After an episode in which Queen Vashti embarrassed her husband, the Persian king, in front of his associates, he issued a decree for all the virgins to come to the palace so that he could choose a new queen (Esther 2:1–4). Esther was one of the virgins taken to the palace. King Xerxes liked her the most, however, his most powerful official, Haman, didn't care for Mordecai's attitude toward him. When Haman found out Mordecai was Jewish, Haman, out of anger and resentment, concocted a plan to kill every Jewish person in Xerxes's empire (Esther 3:6). Hate for people causes people to make some pretty dumb decisions.

Instead of targeting Mordecai alone, Haman wanted to wipe out every person who was Jewish. Haman was a descendant of Agag, the king of the Amalekites. The Amalekites were long-time enemies of the Israelites. Mordecai didn't want to bow to Haman because Mordecai was a god-fearing Jewish man—even if he was comfortably living in a pagan land.

Mordecai found out about Haman's scheme and told Esther. Mordecai strongly reminded Esther that she, herself, was of Jewish descent, and just because they kept her nationality a secret didn't mean she wasn't going to be found out (Esther 4:12–14). Maybe this initially caused Esther to fear for her own life, but moments later, her self-centered thoughts turned outward. Suddenly, it became about everyone else but her. How do we know she put her life aside for others? Because the Bible says so.

> Then Esther sent this reply to Mordecai: "Go, gather together all the Jews who are in Susa, and fast for me. Do not eat or drink for three days, night or day. I and my attendants will fast as you do. When this is done, I will go to the king, even though it is against the law. And if I perish, I perish."
>
> —ESTHER 4:15–16

Esther rallied Mordecai to gather the people to fast and pray, and she said she would also rally her people inside the palace. She never said to go around town and bad mouth Haman. She never spoke about a plan to wage war personally against Haman. Instead, she told Mordecai to humble himself before God and she would do the same. During the three days they all prayed and fasted, God's plan unfolded, and Esther took action. This action was dangerous because she put her life on the line to save all the Jews. She went into the king uninvited. Going before the presence of the king without an invitation could have meant her death. But as I mentioned before, the king loved Esther the most, and she found favor with him. Eventually,

Haman's plan unraveled and Haman was exposed. The king ordered Haman's execution upon the gallows Haman built for Mordecai (Esther 7:9–10).

The part of this story that has always interested me is the fact the Jewish people still had to go to war. God didn't miraculously lift the orders that Haman sent out throughout the kingdom. The enemies still came against the Jewish people and they were told to defend themselves, but God was fighting for and with them. The Jewish people survived because Esther cared enough about her people to risk her life. She cared enough to fast, pray, and wait on God for a plan, as well as His help.

Most often today, our first response is not to tear our clothes, put on burlap, cover ourselves with ashes, pray, and fast. Instead, we turn to social media to vent our anger, sorrow, and frustration to people who can't move mountains. If we grow accustomed to seeking the counsel or approval of people before we seek the Lord, we run the risk of relying on manmade opinions instead of seeking the heart of the Father. Just because we think we have all the answers or we think we can provide for ourselves, the fact is God is the One who holds all the answers and the world in His hands. He loves His creation more than anyone. It's why God sent Jesus to save the world.

When our new normal response to all the wrongs in this world is to fall to our knees and seek the face of God, the world and everything around us can and will change. When our response to all the wrongs in this world is to type out a post or post a story on Facebook or Instagram, we run the risk of stirring up trouble instead of being a part of the solution. Despite what some would have you think, God does answer prayers. He answers prayers for those wrapped up in sin, for those rebelling against God, for broken marriages, for prisoners, for the morally bankrupt, for the ones secretly sinning, for wayward children, for acts of violence against mankind, for poverty, and for so much more. These prayers can change a generation—this generation—if we will take the time to be faithful and persistent in prayer. When you pray the Father's heart, hearts will change, including your own.

We often become the reason nonbelievers turn from God. Sometimes it is a glance, a shuffling in the seat when someone unfamiliar walks into church and sits beside you, a conversation overheard over coffee or lunch or a social media post made in haste or poor judgment. It's not their fault; it is ours. Our prejudices against those who are walking outside of a relationship with Christ reveal themselves when we don't see immediate repentance and salvation. We don't realize that it sometimes takes time for people to watch how we live and treat others before their hardened hearts become hearts of flesh and receptive to the love of Christ.

To love like Christ is to love for the long haul, because I believe Jesus mourns for the eternal death of all those who never choose to follow Him. Our goal as Christ followers should be to love like Jesus and to live lives of obedience. Just as Paul wrote to the believers in Rome, we can't teach them if we are unteachable. We can't tell them not to sin if we ourselves continue to sin. We cannot obtain perfection in our own strength, but the Holy Spirit in us changes our hearts, including our hearts toward those who need Him as their Father. May more people praise the name of Jesus because of the things you do and the way you love rather than blaspheme His great name (Rom. 2:24).

Friend, you and I have much work to do in this world. There are spiritual orphans everywhere. They are hurting, lonely, sad, angry, depressed, and misguided—even if they don't think they are. Some are committing heinous acts and horrific crimes. Some are hurting groups of people simply because that's what they've been told to do. And others, well, they are "good" people but don't know Jesus.

Be the hands and feet of Jesus and help this generation. Intercede for this generation. The Lord can heal our land, but it first starts with people. Love people where they are until they can figure out who they are in Christ. That's what someone did for you, so do it for someone—many someones—over and over until God calls you to your heavenly home. This world will be much better for it. Our godless generation will only be saved from our current crisis by a major turn back to God. Be a light bearer and show them the way.

Advocating for the Spiritual Orphan

1. What has grace meant to you personally?

2. Is there a sect of society you are unwilling to witness to? Why or why not?

3. Why do you think Jesus would hang on a cross in between two criminals? What does that mean for us today?

4. How is God asking you to use any pain you have experienced as your platform to reach spiritual orphans?

5. Why do you think it is hard to love people where they are? What if it takes them years before they finally accept Jesus? Then what?

Chapter Nine

WE ARE THE CATALYST

D AVE PHILLIPS, A dear friend and founder of Children's Hunger Fund, felt the call to help the least at a young age. As a twenty-something newly married young man, he quit his job and told his wife, Lynn, that he was going to start a ministry. They stepped out in faith, and the ministry was birthed. Their garage served as the initial distribution hub. Family and friends gathered together to distribute food and other goods to those in need within their community.

Not long into their ministry, the Northridge earthquake struck California. God allowed Dave Phillips and Children's Hunger Fund to meet the needs of those in their community and from that point, Children's Hunger Fund has continued to soar. It serves those in the United States, reaches the nations, and responds to humanitarian crisis all around the world.

In 2016, as the organization celebrated twenty-five years of ministry, Dave told the story of an encounter with a young man who served as a reminder of the role of the local church in loving those who are lost and have not been reached by the saving grace of the gospel.

In the regular course of business, Dave was visiting the bank. As he exited, the assistant manager called after him, "Mr. Phillips!"

Dave turned around, and the young man asked if he had a minute and could they sit together.

As they sat, the banker said, "You don't recognize me, do you? My name is Herman."

Herman grew up in Pacoima, a very poor part of the San Fernando Valley in Southern California. It also happens to be the location of the first Children's Hunger Fund distribution center. Herman shared that when he was a young teenager, he had a single mom who abused drugs. He, himself, was a drug runner for a local gang. One day, a volunteer from a local church brought food to their home. His mom was never around, but she found out about the food and somehow discovered that it came from Children's Hunger Fund, which was right down the street.

Herman's mom had encouraged him to go down the street to the distribution center to see if he could volunteer. Surprised, he asked her why. She replied that maybe Children's Hunger Fund would give him more food, or perhaps he could even just take some food or other resources while he was volunteering. So, Herman volunteered on a Saturday morning and then returned a second time.

He reminisced that each time he came to volunteer, Dave would always share at the end of each volunteer event that the reason Children's Hunger Fund did what it did was to deliver hope to children in need. Dave said every time, "The one true hope, the best hope we have, is through a relationship with Jesus Christ."

Herman said, "Dave, something happened when I volunteered a second time and heard that message repeated. Something told me I could trust that and I needed to check that out." He continued, "That original volunteer kept coming back to our home, and we started asking questions. Then we got involved in the church. Everything changed, and now here I am, working at this bank."

Dave rejoiced, saying how encouraged he was to see what God had done. But Herman hadn't come to the end of his story.

"Dave," he exclaimed, "you don't know the half of it! That was twenty years ago."

Herman gave glory to God for blessing him with a godly wife and three beautiful kids. He told Dave that he was the youth pastor at his church. Herman credited the church volunteers that came to his home twenty years prior not only with food but also with the message he heard reiterated by the volunteers and during the volunteer events at Children's Hunger Fund. The message was delivered with kindness and compassion. There is incredible power in the gospel to transform lives and the incredible importance of the local church (made up of people). The church is God's instrument for reaching the lost. It's by design.

Throughout the history of Children's Hunger Fund, Dave has relied on God to provide. He, along with his family, incredible staff, and amazing volunteers and partnerships with local churches around the world, have reached out with kindness to people in need. Food is always delivered with the gospel message because Dave knows food can only carry a person so far. They deliver hope wrapped in a Food Pak.

Maybe you and I aren't taking a Food Pak to someone today, but there are needs all around us. Sometimes your presence is all someone needs. Maybe it is a ride to a doctor's appointment. Or perhaps babysitting services for a single mom. Whatever it is, don't allow the physical need to overshadow the spiritual need. I think about Herman's story. What if he had only received food from the volunteers and nothing else? Perhaps he would have ventured deeper into a life of drugs and crime. Maybe he would have died young. Food only sustained him for a few hours, but the gospel of Jesus Christ saved his life and changed his life. God is good.

I began writing this book in May 2017 shortly after the bombings at the Ariana Grande concert at the Manchester Arena in the United Kingdom I mentioned in chapter five. It amazes me that in less than two years (as of the date of this writing), our attention has shifted so much. In 2017, America, as well as many parts of the world, feared ISIS, our greatest threat at the time. We feared the hate they had for western ways. We feared when the next bombing might take place and where that might occur. Fear turned to anger and outrage. Fear denounced ISIS's religion, which appeared to be the driving force behind their hatred. However, even as fear gripped us, Jesus pursued and is still pursuing ISIS leaders in the wilderness. There is no stopping an all-powerful and mighty God.

What I also find ironic is that in less than two years, Americans have gone from hating and fearing ISIS because of the death they bring to shouting that death through abortion is an OK and acceptable choice. How can we despise death and embrace it at the same time? ISIS news stories no longer headline the front page in America (although they often do around the rest of the world). Instead, abortion as a choice, abortion as a right, and that up to the moment of delivery, abortion is not murder appear in the headline news. However ironic it is, if a baby at a café, a concert, on the side of a road, or kidnapped in hostile territory was killed by ISIS, the world would cry, "Murder! Terrorist! Evil!"

I agree this would all be true of ISIS, yet, is it not the same in our American acceptance of abortion? Even the eleven unborn children who died at the hands of terrorists in 1993 and on September 11, 2001, at the Twin Towers in New York are recognized as lives lost on the memorial.[44] We mourn and memorialize the loss of unborn life taken at the hands of extremists during those two events in New York City. However, in that same city, the governor, along with hundreds (maybe even thousands), cheered when legislation passed recently to allow women the right to terminate a pregnancy up until the ninth month.[45]

A CNN article dated February 12, 2018, claims that ISIS is responsible for one hundred and forty-three attacks resulting in the deaths of two thousand forty-three people worldwide.[46] Contrast this to the over one-and-half billion (and counting by the second) babies aborted worldwide since 1980 (not even 1973 after *Roe v. Wade*), and ISIS does not seem like the enemy we should fear the most. The foundation of both ideologies behind these movements is a failure to obey the command Jesus laid out for the world, "Love."

Radical ISIS members, according to their Islamic faith, believe they are serving the One True God, and that their god demands the death of all those who oppose him. While in a way this is true (eternal death will result in those who oppose God), God never asks us to take the matter of death into our own hands. He is, was, and will always be God. God is the one who gets to sit on the throne of judgment and make the decision about who loves Him and who does not love Him. Not us.

Instead, Jesus gave the Great Commission in Matthew 28:19 instructing His followers to go and make disciples and baptize them in the name of the Father, Son, and Holy Spirit. He never said to kill those who oppose you, inconvenience you, or have other beliefs. Jesus knew the only solution for wayward souls was love because loving God sets people on a path to fearing God, which is the beginning of knowledge.[47] Knowledge of what? The heart of God.

Every January 27 is a day of remembrance of the liberation at Auschwitz. While the Holocaust is a complicated and sensitive event in the history of our world, there is so much more we can learn from the Holocaust than most consider. So much more. It's not just about being worried about insane leaders; it is also about the choice that each one of us makes to say yes to Jesus. Did you know that the majority of the Jewish people killed in the Holocaust were Ashkenazi Jews? These Jews were thought to have been pushed out of the Roman Empire when Christianity was the driving force of that day. Makes sense, right? The apostles were evangelizing, and people were becoming Christians. But as we know from reading the Bible, many didn't believe.

As the Ashkenazi Jews fled Rome, they migrated to places like Germany, Poland, Yugoslavia, and Ireland. A lot of the Ashkenazi Jews killed during the Holocaust had German, Polish, and/or Irish in their blood because races intermingled over the years. They still do today (including me, at a very small percentage).

> During World War II, about six million Jews, five million of whom were Ashkenazi, were killed in the Holocaust. The Holocaust destroyed or greatly reduced the large Jewish communities and the Yiddish language in Europe. Many of the surviving Ashkenazi Jews emigrated to countries such as Israel, Canada, Argentina, Australia, and the United States after the war. Today Ashkenazim are 80 percent of Jews of the world.[48]

This thought may be upsetting and controversial to some, but we often try and place the blame on one single person for all of society's wrongs instead of looking individually at our internal rebellion against God.

What if the Ashkenazi Jews had given their lives to Jesus and remained in Rome? Would the Holocaust have ever happened? Satan is deceptive, and he waits for open doors of opportunity. Satan used Hitler's insecurity, pride, and hatred to wipe out millions. But we can't forget about the sovereignty of God. Remember Job? Satan had to ask permission from God to wreck his life. Remember Pharaoh? God had him in a position of power for a reason. There were times of peace and prosperity in the Old Testament. Do you know when? When the people were obedient to God and following His ways. Anytime they strayed from these two things, it never worked out.

Both ISIS and abortion—among so many other issues of today—are deep spiritual issues manifesting in the physical realm. Why is ISIS a group? Because like I said above, their theology is wrong. Why do people abort babies or believe abortion is OK? People have sex outside of marriage and aren't ready to handle the consequence of that choice. There are rapists with serious issues hurting women and leaving a path of destruction in their wake. People have hard choices because babies are not knit together in the same manner within the womb and babies might be born with serious health complications. Not all babies are wanted by the people who play a part in making them. I cannot imagine the thoughts and demons plaguing people who find themselves struggling with the choice to abort a baby. I empathize with them, and I mourn for them.

Instead of beating down the person making the decision, how can we, as a society, and individually, as the hands and feet of Jesus, help redefine the sanctity and preciousness of life—all life? The story of our generation could be written into the pages of the Old Testament. And I am not talking about the stories of nations bowing to God and living in prosperity and peace. I am talking about the stories plagued with chaos, death, and destruction. How I so badly want to change the story for our generation. Lord, have mercy on us today. I don't know about you, but I am watching things change so quickly in this country as people rebel against God. What might God do to our generation?

We are battling the legalization of abortion at any stage during a pregnancy (which started at the evil hands of one lady, Margaret Sanger, who wanted to wipe out the black race through abortion).[49] We are quickly sinking in the sand of same-sex marriage and transgenderism (and no gender for that matter) thanks to the millions of dollars secretly and silently pumped into politics, schools, media, and television by billionaires of whom nobody knows much about, Paul Singer,[50] Tim Gill,[51] and Daniel Loeb.[52] These people were used/are being used as instruments of evil by Satan (self-professed hatred, and anger). We have scandals raging in every sector of business and entertainment. Politicians can't stand to work with one another. People are abusing and killing children of all ages. The list goes on and on.

Some may not believe it or buy into (even some well-meaning Christians), but Jesus is the answer—the only answer—to ushering in heaven on Earth before He returns to gather His bride. His love and grace are free gifts to those who believe. As we love Him, Jesus says that our obedience follows.[53] We must help spiritual orphans know this love so they can hear from the Spirit as to what is wrong and what is right in the eyes of the Lord. It's only His conviction that changes a person's heart completely.

My belief in the infallible Word of God does not make me someone who hates those who live opposed to God's Word; it makes me feel sorry for them that they either don't know the love of Jesus or are still rejecting His love. It makes me want to ask the Holy Spirit to use my life and whatever influence He gives me to speak life into people who need Jesus. May He use my voice as of voice of encouragement and truth in the wilderness the spiritual orphan and rebellious find themselves in, as well as to those who call themselves Christians but don't live love.

I hate death, violence, and conflict, but lives depend on the truth, and I can't stand by and watch my children's generation—biological and spiritual—be led to slaughter on my watch. Charles G. Finney said, "Revivals are hindered when ministers and churches take wrong ground in regard to any question involving human rights."[54] He was addressing the issue of slavery in America, but he knew then, "It is doubtless true that one of the reasons for the low state of religion at the present time is that many churches have taken the wrong side on the subject of slavery, have suffered prejudice to prevail over principle, and have feared to call this abomination by its true name."

There are many abominations in America today deserving of calling out and addressing both within and outside the church. How we approach those wrapped up in sin and blind to the truth—both spiritual orphans and prodigals—will be the catalyst for change. We must not find ourselves in what Dr. Michael Brown said about

Finney's prediction: "If a spiritual awakening did not come first, then the battle over slavery would end with a bloody war."[55] The only blood we need to cover our land in this generation is the blood of Jesus.

May we—you and I—bind up everything blinding eyes and hardening hearts of people today, and may we loose the Spirit of the living God into the hearts of people in this nation. May we be people after God's own heart. As our hearts change, things will change. I am praying the headlines we begin to see are about life and no longer all about death. Will you join me?

> Truly I [Jesus] tell you, whatever you bind on earth will be bound in heaven, and whatever you loose on earth will be loosed in heaven. Again, truly I tell you that if two of you on earth agree about anything they ask for, it will be done for them by my Father in heaven.
>
> —MATTHEW 18:18–19

Advocating for the Spiritual Orphan

1. How do you feel when you read the headline news?

2. What are the ways God is calling you to step in and help this generation?

3. Have you been an active participant in the Great Commission?

4. Are you speaking up about the things that matter to God?

5. Will you commit to reaching more spiritual orphans?

FOR THE ORPHAN—YOUR ADOPTION PLAN

This section is dedicated to those who don't yet know Jesus. If you know Him, feel free to skip this section, but I can't finish this book without adding these words to those who may not know Jesus as their Savior.

I AM NOT SURE how you stumbled upon this book. Perhaps someone gave it to you. Maybe you saw it online or on a shelf and the front cover grabbed your attention. I don't know, but regardless, know that I have prayed for you. If you get nothing else out of this book, I want you to know that Jesus loves you. You are not alone in this world even if it feels like you are right at this very moment. If you have no one else in this world to turn to right now, please know you have a God in heaven who wants to be your Father. God is a father whose love is unlike any love you will ever experience by a person on this Earth. God is love (1 John 4:8). Regardless of what you have done or not done up until this moment in time, God knows it all. But even though He knows it all, He sees you through what you can become instead of who you are right now.

Not too long ago, I witnessed my dear friends officially adopt a baby boy they were blessed with just two months ago. The whole thing came as a surprise to them (and to me). The birth mother was unable to care for her baby and made the decision to relinquish her rights. Fortunately, she had help placing the baby with a family who would care for her baby.

It's not a perfect system by any means, but it reminds me that even in this not-so-perfect world, good things can happen. And the best thing that can happen to any one of us is that we allow ourselves to be adopted into God's family, the Father who loves us and prays for us more than any physical human being.

> God sets the lonely in families, he leads out the prisoners with singing; but the rebellious live in a sun-scorched land.
>
> —PSALM 68:6

God created the heavens and the earth and everyone and everything on the earth. He sustains life, seasons, and order. He is awesome and worthy to be praised. The problem is, so many people throughout history have failed to honor God, and only God. Every rule God put in place was simply a way of protecting us. He knows what sin can do to each one of us. As a Father, He wants only the best for you and for all His children. We need His instruction to keep us safe on the path of life. Without His guardrails, we can fall off into who knows what with who knows what in the miry mud.

His unfailing love continues forever, and His faithfulness continues to each generation.

—PSALM 100:5

In Luke 16:19–31, Jesus spoke of the parable of the rich man and Lazarus. Lazarus led a life no one would have wanted. Lazarus was a poor man who laid day by day at the gate of a rich man. Lazarus was covered in sores, and all he wanted was to be fed with the scraps that fell from the rich man's table. He was in such a sad state that even the dogs came and licked his sores, but the rich man did nothing to help this poor man.

Both men died and one was carried to the side of Abraham in heaven and one was taken down to Hades. The rich man had everything he ever needed in this life, but the poor man was always in need. It was in death the poor man found everything he needed. The rich man, however, had everything he thought he ever needed when he was alive, but in death, he yearned for comfort and reprieve from his anguish. The rich man couldn't find any relief because of the great chasm between eternal life in heaven and eternal life in hell.

The rich man was so distraught that he thought of his living brothers and begged Abraham to go to his brothers to tell them how to get to heaven so they wouldn't live a life of torment. Abraham, however, said that they had already received the word of testimony from Abraham and the prophets, and that their stubborn hearts and deaf ears wouldn't allow them to hear the words anyway.

You, my friend, must heed the words of the testimony. If you haven't already done so, you must make a choice whether you are going to accept or reject Jesus as the Savior of the world and more importantly, as *your* personal Savior. Every person must do this. The Bible says, "Today, if you hear his voice, do not harden your heart as you did in the rebellion" (Heb. 3:15).

Long ago, the prophet Isaiah delivered messages about the coming Messiah and these prophecies were fulfilled in the person of Jesus Christ. John 3:16 says, "For God so loved the world that He gave His only begotten Son that whosoever believes in Him shall not perish but have eternal life." God loves the world, and this includes every single person living in it. Throughout history, God gave those who were not originally part of the chosen ones the opportunity to forsake all their other gods and to honor only God. Some made the right choice, but many did not. Nothing good comes from denying God. Nothing.

God sent His remedy to the world—Jesus, who was born, lived, died, and rose again. Many people of all religions and ethnicities agree that Jesus was a man who lived, however, some don't see Him as the Savior. They either are bowing down to some other savior or waiting for a savior, but their waiting will be in vain because the Savior has not only come, but He will also one day come again.

Jesus gave up His crown on this Earth so that you could be adopted into His family and called royalty. I know, it might sound too good to be true. You may not feel royal, special, or even worthy, but the great thing about God is that it doesn't always matter what we feel or say about ourselves. Our worth and value are found in who He says we are. He calls us loved, chosen, and precious. God calls us His children and no longer spiritual orphans when we finally say yes to Him. He grants us peace and joy beyond anything we can attain on our own through the power of the Holy Spirit.

> For he chose us in him before the creation of the world to be holy and blameless in his sight. In love he predestined us for adoption to sonship through Jesus Christ, in accordance with his pleasure and will.
>
> —EPHESIANS 1:4–5

The world may say you have no family or have no worth, but that is simply not true. You have a family larger than you can fathom and the greatest Father imaginable. Some orphans don't have a choice in who their family is, but you, spiritual orphan, get to choose. And choose you must.

You Must Make a Choice

It's OK to ask the hard questions as you seek the Lord. At just the right time, when the Holy Spirit tugs at your heart, you'll be ready to take a deep breath and knock at the door (I am praying right now that you are ready). Tap the door lightly or pound it loudly—either way, Jesus will open it and let you in (Matt. 7:8).

Perhaps you have heard about God and Jesus before. Maybe someone even shared the gospel message with you. It's hard to understand, but sometimes it just isn't our time to hear it or respond positively. You see, salvation cannot be forced. Why? Because God, not people, is in charge. In John 6:44 Jesus said, "No one can come to me unless the Father who sent me draws them." Salvation wasn't on your mind first, but it has always been on God's mind. He loves you that much.

I'm pretty sure someone has hurt you before. Hurt isn't always physical. It can be emotional or verbal. People are faulty, and people make mistakes. Even good people say things they shouldn't say. If someone has hurt you or disappointed you, know that it has not gone unseen. God is omniscient, meaning He sees it all. He hurts when you hurt. He hurts when you make bad choices. Jesus prays for you (Rom. 8:34). Imagine that. Maybe you have never thought that a single person on this planet ever prayed for you. Even if no one on Earth prays for you, Jesus does.

The Bible says we are all born into sin, and because of sin, we are separated from God. The only way we can be united with God is through a sacrifice. Jesus was that sacrifice for all of mankind until the new age. The saddest thing for me is that so many people will assume they get a free pass to heaven or their "next life" by doing absolutely nothing or at best, being a "good" person. None of us are good enough. We can't work our way into heaven because we all fall short (Rom. 3:23). Grace is what God offers, and it is a free gift that requires a step of faith to believe in and say yes to Jesus (Eph. 2:8).

If you are tired of struggling in this world and feeling alone, surrender to Jesus today. Maybe you have everything you need in this world, including people and possessions, but you still feel like something is missing. That something is Jesus. The One who created you and knit you together created you to desire Him, not because He is proud but because He is love. He needed us to desire Him so that we could cling to Him to walk through this life on the right path.

God didn't sin. Man (and woman) sinned because of free will. God gave Adam and Eve specific instructions to follow, and they chose to do the thing God told them not to do. You and I are still suffering the consequences of their sinful choice. However, by the grace of God, those of us living today have a chance to receive God's forgiveness and be reconciled with Him because of Jesus. We do this through faith and by receiving His free gift of salvation (Eph. 2:8–9). This salvation includes forgiveness of our sins (past, present, and future). My children didn't get the opportunity to choose me as their mom, but you and I get to choose to ask God to be our Father forever.

So, what choice will your free will make today? Are you tired of being a spiritual orphan searching for something or someone to believe in? If so, I pray you surrender to Jesus today and become my brother or sister in the faith. I may not ever meet you or know you in this lifetime, but I know we will be together in heaven forever.

It's not complicated to surrender to Jesus because He knows your heart. Some will say you need to say certain words or do certain things, but it isn't like that. If He is drawing you to Him, speak to Him. Whatever comes to mind, just speak. You don't have to wait for a church service or for someone to witness your prayer. You can do it right now. He knows honest and humble hearts. He'll hear whatever you say. If you need help, start by saying, "Jesus, help me."

What Do You Do Now?

This afterword has gone one of two ways for you: either you made the choice for eternal life in heaven or you remain seeking and searching. Either way, you still have something to do. If you are still seeking and searching, don't give up. Perhaps you are reading through the Bible to find answers. Keep reading! Maybe you are having conversations with Christians. Keep talking! Maybe you are praying to God for answers. Please keep praying!

As long as you are breathing, you have the opportunity to seek and search. However, don't forget that we are not guaranteed our next breath so consider that when you are seeking.

Are you still seeking because you are scared or don't yet want to give up the pleasures of this world? If so, ask God to take those things from you and see how your heart toward Him changes. Only He can turn your heart of stone into a heart of flesh.

Maybe you made the decision to surrender to Jesus. I am shouting, "Hallelujah!" for you. Heaven roars when one person comes to salvation (Luke 15:7). So now what do you do? Tell someone what you just did. They may or may not understand, but that's OK. Be proud of the biggest decision you will ever make. You never know. The very next person you talk to may need Jesus too.

The gift of salvation is a guarantee for your eternal life but, in this life, biblical community is important for you.

Surround yourself with Bible-believing people who will help you grow, keep you accountable, and help you find your God-given gifts and talents to be used to build up the local church body.

As a born-again believer, you can now access the Holy Spirit who will guide you as He resides within you (1 Cor. 12:7). Make sure you tap into this power by asking God to fill you with the Holy Spirit. Jesus said in Luke 11:13, "If you then, though you are evil, know how to give good gifts to your children, how much more will your Father in heaven give the Holy Spirit to those who ask him!" This Holy Spirit power is the same power that raised Jesus from the dead. Don't let this power go!

Sometimes after the newness of salvation wears off, some people forget who they were before grace appeared. While God forgives at the moment of salvation, the further we get from this moment of grace, the easier it is to forget how bad (or lost) we were before salvation. When we forget who we were and where we came from, it impacts how we see and treat those who are still finding their way to the Father. Please don't ever let the grace you extend wear out. Also, don't let that first-love moment wear off. Remember how you felt the moment you realized what Jesus did for you and how much God loves you? Keep that moment close. Being a Christian isn't always easy, but knowing how much He loves you makes it worth it.

Know also that many times, God will use us to reach the people we can so easily relate to. Were you an addict? Don't be surprised when God gives you an assignment to reach other addicts. Were you an out-of-control prodigal?

Guess who God might be asking you to reach? Were you someone who was angry with God because of stuff that happened in your life? Yes, maybe angry, God-hating people are now your assignment to reach.

God will use us where we were weak because we speak that language of weakness to a specific person or group. Don't be afraid of the challenge. People's lives are depending on it.

If you feel led and if you haven't already, start reading this book from the beginning. It will help you steer clear of making many of the mistakes Christians make. Christians are not called to judge; we are called to love. We are to be an extension of Christ on Earth, and we are told to let our light shine (Matt. 5:16).

Be a light bearer and let the world know that you are no longer a spiritual orphan. Go after the spiritual orphans. You can recognize them because they were you.

About the Author

HONESTLY, NEVER IN her wildest dreams did Erin ever think she would be writing about Jesus. "Really, are you kidding me?" she laughs. But when Jesus gets a hold of your heart, it is hard to let Him go. Without Him, your heart is missing something. You may or may not know what that something is, but when you have Him, you just know.

Erin grew up going to church but was far from what she considers a "church girl." She didn't give much thought to God six days and twenty-three hours per week. She was a "one-hour-a-week church-goer." Nothing more, nothing less. She was fortunate to know who God was, and she accepted what she thought she knew and understood (at least she thought she did). She never doubted for a minute who the Creator was, she just denied Him—*all the time.* She had no idea that He was the Person she had been searching and longing for. "I had no concept of the enormity of the Cross. I knew of God, but I didn't know Jesus," she says.

She made some misguided choices as a teenager and young adult. They scaled in degrees of how misguided they were, but nevertheless, they were not good. As a young, single adult, she moved from Southern California to Dallas, Texas. She didn't know anyone, have a job lined up, and didn't know the best part of town to live in. However, it ended up being a place where she met her husband. Several years after her move to Dallas, she gave her life to Jesus, and her life was forever changed.

Her goal in all she does is to glorify God not herself. We all have a story that is unique to us. "Don't get me wrong, Jesus does not need an opening act by any means," she says, "But what He likes to do best is to use ordinary people to do extraordinary things. He uses the least of us, and often some of the most messed up, to magnify Him."

Even before she knew Jesus, He knew her. "He was pursuing me, and watching for me down the road. At His God-appointed moment, He sent someone to speak a word of knowledge to me. It was a word that only God could have known because the person who said it to me was someone I had never met before. That got my attention and softened my heart. I gave my whole life—not just a piece of it—to Jesus that night even though I didn't have it completely figured out. He didn't need a big, prideful faith. He wanted my humble heart to be healed and filled with His Spirit. I believed, and He freely gave. I've never looked back."

He loves us even when we don't love ourselves—or Him. Never give up hope because He will never give up on you.

What She Does with What She's Been Given

Erin will tell you she is most comfortable in jeans and a T-shirt either writing or having a conversation with someone about the power available to them through Christ and the Holy Spirit. Erin's primary full-time ministry is that of a homemaker, which consists of serving her husband, Scott, three children, three Havanese pups, and their latest addition, a Portidoodle puppy named Esther. Prior to relocating to Birmingham, AL, in June of 2018, Erin volunteered in the women's and children's ministries, taught women's Bible study, and was the director of a Bible fellowship class at her home church in Dallas, TX. She also started and taught Bible studies in her neighborhood, and founded the National Prayer Walk Your Neighborhood in May 2017.

In January 2012, Erin launched her first blog, and her ministry, Sandalfeet Ministries, was birthed. She has been a guest contributor on a number of blogs and is the author of three published works: a ten-week Bible study, *Forgiveness—Unforgiveness: Revealed Through Your Fruits*, a Lent devotional, *Sit at His Feet: Choose What Is Better*, and an Advent devotional, *Simplify the Season: Rediscovering Christ Through Advent*.

In February 2018, Erin launched "Lunchtime Lessons" via Facebook Live (facebook.com/sandalfeet). "Lunchtime Lessons" is a thirty-minute Bible study covering books of the Bible ("Lunchtime Lessons" is also available on her ministry podcast—Sandalfeet Ministries).

Erin serves on the Regional Advisory Team (Dallas) for All In Sports Outreach (allinsportsoutreach.org) and served as a character coach for the girls' sports teams at a middle school in Dallas. There are also many other ministries, missionaries, and children around the world that have a piece of her heart and support.

Prior to staying at home with her children, Erin worked as a corporate/intellectual property paralegal for large firms and corporations for almost a decade.

Erin has a bachelor's degree in business administration from Regis University (Denver, CO) and a master's degree in Christian leadership from Liberty Baptist Theological Seminary (Lynchburg, VA). She is an ordained minister.

Notes

Introduction

1. Mario Vittone and Francesco A. Pita, PhD, "It Doesn't Look Like They're Drowning," *On Scene: The Journal of U.S. Coast Guard Search and Rescue* (Fall 2006):14, http://mariovittone.com/wp-content/uploads/2010/05/OSFall06.pdf.

2. Oxford Dictionaries, s.v. "crisis," https://en.oxforddictionaries.com/definition/crisis.

3. W. Fay and L. E. Shepherd, *Share Jesus without Fear* (Nashville, TN: Broadman & Holman, 1999).

Chapter 1: Remember Where You Came From

1. Carey Nieuwhf, "Why Christians Should Let Non-Christians Off the Moral Hook," CareyNieuwhof.com, https://careynieuwhof.com/why-christians-should-let-non-christians-off-the-moral-hook-2/.

2. Rocha, "2-21: The Significance of the Direction 'East' in the Scriptures," Messianic Revolution, http://messianic-revolution.com/2-21-significance-direction-east-scriptures/

3. Paule. "East of God – West of Man." Valid Ambiguity. December 4, 2015. Accessed 14 February 2019. http://validambiguity.com/2015/12/04/east-of-god/.

4. BlueLetterBible.com, s.v. *"chanowk,"* https://www.blueletterbible.org//lang/lexicon/lexicon.cfm?Strongs=H2585&t=KJV

5. David C. Wright, "Timeline for the Flood," Answers in Genesis, https://answersingenesis.org/bible-timeline/timeline-for-the-flood/.

Chapter 2: Family Baggage

1. G. Whitefield, S. Drew, and J. Smith, *Sermons on Important Subjects* (London: William Tegg, 1867).

2. Freddie García and Ninfa García, *Outcry in the Barrio* (N.p.: Freddy García Ministries, 1987).

3. Ibid.

4. Bob Goff, *Everybody Always* (Nashville, TN: Thomas Nelson, 2018).

Chapter 3: The Call

1. Franz Kafka, "The Fathers of the Church were not afraid to go out into the desert because they had a richness in their hearts. But we..." QuoteFancy.com, https://quotefancy.com/quote/807045/Franz-Kafka-The-Fathers-of-the-Church-were-not-afraid-to-go-out-into-the-desert-because

2. Maria Pasquini, "Lauren Daigle Claps Back After Being Criticized for Performing on Ellen DeGeneres' Show," People.com, November 2, 2018, https://people.com/music/lauren-daigle-claps-back-ellen-degeneres-show-criticism/.

3. Merriam-Webster.com, s.v. "hypocrite," https://www.merriam-webster.com/dictionary/hypocrite.

4. Merriam-Webster.com, s.v. "revive," https://www.merriam-webster.com/dictionary/revive.

5. Lisa Bevere, *Without Rival* (Grand Rapids, MI: Revell, 2016).

6. Natalie Stephens Herrington, *The Forgotten Ones* (N.p.: Mackenzie Publishing, 2017).

Chapter 4: Remember the Mission

1. BibleHub.com, s.v. "Matthew 1:5," https://biblehub.com/commentaries/matthew/1-5.htm.

2. BibleStudyTools.com, s.v. *"yathowm,"* http://www.biblestudytools.com/lexicons/hebrew/kjv/yathowm.html.

3. "Statistics," April 27, 2010, https://thefatherlessgeneration.wordpress.com/statistics/.

4. "Ping Pong," *M.A.S.H., directed by William K. Jergenson* (1977, Los Angeles, CA: 20th Century Fox Television), https://www.imdb.com/title/tt0638384/?ref_=ttep_ep16.

5. Acts 2

6. Matthew 28:19

7. R. F. Capon, *Kingdom, Grace, Judgment Paradox, Outrage, and Vindication in the Parables of Jesus* (Grand Rapids, MI: Eerdmans, 2002).

Chapter 5: Change Your Language

1. Rick Gladstone and Dan Bilefsky, "Insidious Twist on Terror Attack Victims: Teens and Young Girls with Mothers in Tow," *New York Times*, May 23, 2017, http://www.nytimes.com/2017/05/23/world/europe/manchester-bombing-victims.html?action=click&contentCollection=Europe&module=RelatedCoverage%C2%AEion&pgtype=article.

2. Kurt Schlichter, "Fewer Tears, Fewer Lies, And More Righteous Anger," Townhall.com, May 25, 2017, https://townhall.com/columnists/kurtschlichter/2017/05/25/fewer-tears-fewer-lies-and-more-righteous-anger-n2331247.

3. Jennifer Eivaz and Kris Vallotton, *The Intercessors Handbook* (Minneapolis, MN: Chosen, 2016).

4. Anne Graham Lotz, Facebook.com, March 26, 2015, https://www.facebook.com/AnneGrahamLotz/photos/a.10151085215612476/10152955031692476/?type=1&theater.

Chapter 6: Windows to Our Souls

1. Gilbert Rogin, "Albie Pearson: The Littlest Angel," Vault, May 27, 1963, https://www.si.com/vault/1963/05/27/595012/albie-pearson-the-littlest-angel.

2. Bill Shaikin, "Hit by a Bombshell," LATimes.com, December 14, 1997, http://articles.latimes.com/1997/dec/14/sports/sp-64080.

3. Marcia C. Smith, "Former Angel Albie Pearson Heard a Higher Calling," Orange County Register Online, April 9, 2011, https://www.ocregister. com/2011/04/09/former-angel-albie-pearson-heard-a-higher-calling/.

Chapter 7: Identify the Enemy

1. Dave Earley and David Wheeler, *Evangelism Is* (Nashville, TN: B & H Publishing Group, 2014), 38.

2. "High-Energy X-ray View of 'Hand of God,'" Jet Propulsion Laboratory, January 9, 2014, https://www.jpl.nasa.gov/spaceimages/details. php?id=pia17566.

3. Tony Greicius, "High-Energy X-ray View of 'Hand of God,'" NASA.gov, https://www.nasa.gov/ jpl/nustar/B1509-pia17566.

4. Bob Goff, Instagram.com, October 5, 2018, https://www.instagram.com/p/Boi7qVrHubn/?utm_ source=ig_web_copy_link. Accessed November 13, 2018.

5. I Am Second, iamsecond.org.

Chapter 8: Focus on Eternal Things

1. Michael Gryboski, "Church Conducts 'Adults Only' Services for Sex Offenders," ChristianPost. com, March 19, 2012, https://www.christianpost. com/news/church-conducts-adults-only-services-for-sex-offenders-others-71695/.

2. "Facts and Stats," LaurensKids.org, https://lauren-skids.org/awareness/about-faqs/facts-and-stats/.

3. Anne Voskamp as quoted by Amy Groe-schel, "Living Worthy of Our Call," The Call: Day 1, Bible.com, https://my.bible.com/reading-plans/12742-the-call/day/1.

4. Dictionary.dom, s.v. "haole," https://www.dic-tionary.com/browse/haole.

5. E. Michael Rusten and Sharon O. Rusten, *The One Year of Christian History* (Wheaton, IL: Tyn-dale House, 2003), 202–203.

Chapter 9: We Are the Catalyst

1. Patrick Kingsley, *"The Jidhadi Who Turned to Jesus,"* New York Times, March 24, 2017, https://www.nytimes.com/2017/03/24/world/middleeast/the-jihadi-who-turned-to-jesus.html.

2. Emily Ngo, "911 Memorial Honors Unborn Babies," Newsday.com, September 11, 2011, https://www.newsday.com/911-anniversary/9-11-memorial-honors-unborn-babies-1.3138677.

3. Bethany Bump, "Cuomo Signs Reproductive Health Act after Legislature Votes," TimesUnion.com, January 22, 2019, https://www.timesunion.com/news/article/New-York-lawmakers-to-vote-on-abortion-rights-13551825.php.

4. Tim Lister et al., "ISIS Goes Global: 143 Attacks in 29 Countries Have Killed 2,043," CNN.com, February 12, 2018, https://www.cnn.

com/2015/12/17/world/mapping-isis-attacks-around-the-world/index.html.

5. Proverbs 9:10.

6. Wikipedia.com, s.v. "Ashkenazi Jews, https://en.m.wikipedia.org/wiki/Ashkenazi_Jews.

7. ACLJ.org, "The Real Margaret Sanger (Planned Parenthood's Founder) Will Shock You," June 2017, https://aclj.org/pro-life/the-real-margaret-sanger-planned-parenthoods-founder-will-shock-you.

8. Ryan Sorba, "Paul Singer's Gay Agenda: Punish, Pay-Off, and Promote," May 3, 2017, http://ryansorba.blogspot.com/2017/05/paul-singers-gay-agenda-punish-pay-off.html.

9. Andy Kroll, "Meet the Megadonor Behind the LGBTQ Rights Movement," Rolling Stone, June 23, 2018, https://www.rollingstone.com/politics/politics-features/meet-the-megadonor-behind-the-lgbtq-rights-movement-193996/amp/.

10. Michael J. De La Merced, "2 Wall Street Moguls Champion Gay Rights," New York Times Online, January 23, 2014, https://dealbook.nytimes.com/2014/01/23/wall-street-talks-gay-rights-at-davos/.

11. John 1:4

12. Charles G. Finney, "Lectures on Revivals of Religion: Hindrances to Revivals," http://www.

charlesgfinney.com/1868Lect_on_Rev_of_
Rel/68revlec15.htm.

13. Michael Brown, "Either Awakening or Civil
War in America over Abortion," AFA.net, February 5, 2019, https://www.afa.net/the-stand/
culture/2019/02/either-awakening-or-civil-war-in-
america-over-abortion/?fbclid=IwAR3hWo7siatGE
4ZWfX7ADSzQahWO_5xPDEaZTdDvKrq65a0T-_
CD1yoWwOw#.XFmmW4-Jhjw.facebook.

CPSIA information can be obtained
at www.ICGtesting.com
Printed in the USA
FSHW011838230619
59349FS

9 780999 354476